797,885 Books
are available to read at

www.ForgottenBooks.com

Forgotten Books' App
Available for mobile, tablet & eReader

ISBN 978-1-332-07017-6
PIBN 10280039

This book is a reproduction of an important historical work. Forgotten Books uses state-of-the-art technology to digitally reconstruct the work, preserving the original format whilst repairing imperfections present in the aged copy. In rare cases, an imperfection in the original, such as a blemish or missing page, may be replicated in our edition. We do, however, repair the vast majority of imperfections successfully; any imperfections that remain are intentionally left to preserve the state of such historical works.

Forgotten Books is a registered trademark of FB &c Ltd.
Copyright © 2015 FB &c Ltd.
FB &c Ltd, Dalton House, 60 Windsor Avenue, London, SW19 2RR.
Company number 08720141. Registered in England and Wales.

For support please visit www.forgottenbooks.com

1 MONTH OF FREE READING

at
www.ForgottenBooks.com

By purchasing this book you are eligible for one month membership to ForgottenBooks.com, giving you unlimited access to our entire collection of over 700,000 titles via our web site and mobile apps.

To claim your free month visit: www.forgottenbooks.com/free280039

* Offer is valid for 45 days from date of purchase. Terms and conditions apply.

Similar Books Are Available from www.forgottenbooks.com

A Study of English Words
by Jessie Macmillan Anderson

How to Write Clearly
Rules and Exercises on English Composition, by Edwin Abbott

Grammar of the English Sentence
by Jonathan Rigdon

Mistakes Writing English, How to Avoid Them
by Marshall T. Bigelow

A Higher English Grammar
by Alexander Bain

Words and Sentences
by Harry Stuart Vedder Jones

McGraw-Hill Handbook of English
by Virginia Shaffer

Better English for Speaking and Writing
A Series of Three Books, by Sarah Emma Simons and Clem Irwin Orr

The Old and Middle English
by Thomas Laurence Kington Oliphant

Advanced Course of Composition and Rhetoric
by G. P. Quackenbos

Everyday English, Vol. 1
by Franklin T. Baker

A Guide to Good English
by Robert Palfrey Utter

An Outline of English Phonetics
by Daniel Jones

Course in General Linguistics
by Ferdinand de Saussure

A Concise Etymological Dictionary of the English Language
by Walter W. Skeat

Pure English
A Treatise on Words and Phrases, or Practical Lessons in the Use of Language, by Fred H. Hackett

English Pronunciation for Foreigners
by Sarah Jan Barrows

Linguistic Change
An Introduction to the Historical Study of Language, by E. H. Sturtevant

An Improved Grammar of the English Language
by Noah Webster

The Excitement of Verbal Adventure, Vol. 1
A Study of Vladimir Nabokov's English Prose, by Jürgen Bodenstein

THE STUDY OF IDYLLS OF THE KING

CRITICAL NOTES, REFERENCES, AND TOPICS FOR STUDY

BY

H. A. DAVIDSON

The Study Guide Series
Cambridge, Mass.

C 18747

CONTENTS.

The Study of Literary Art in Idylls of the King	3
The Distinction between Idyll and Idyllic	54, 63
Directions for Note-book Work	10
Note-book Topics for Classes and for Study-clubs	12
Note-book Topics for Critical Study	13
The Use of the Text	15
The Reading of Criticism	15
Written Papers in Study Clubs	16
Written Work for Advanced Students	17
References for Study of Idylls of the King	18
Topics for Study, with Critical Notes	23
Preliminary	23
For The Coming of Arthur	27
For Gareth and Lynette	32
For Geraint and Enid	37
For Balin and Balan	46
For Merlin and Vivien	50
For Lancelot and Elaine	56
For The Holy Grail	67
For Pelleas and Ettarre	75
For The Last Tournament	79
For Guinevere	83
For The Passing of Arthur	87

Copyright, 1901, 1907, by
H. A. DAVIDSON, M. A., Author of The Creative Art
of Fiction, Literary Study for Busy People,
The Study-Guide Series, etc.

# THE STUDY OF IDYLLS OF THE KING

INTRODUCTION.

THE STUDY OF LITERARY ART IN IDYLLS OF THE KING.

Tennyson's *Idylls of the King* are subtly difficult and complex, full of delicate æsthetic beauty, of noble truth, and pure imagination. In them idyllic and epic qualities intermingle, and the slow evolution of the dramatic story is accomplished through the medium of separate idyllic narratives. The selection and adaptation of old legends and traditions; the elusive infusion of ethical meaning everywhere; the study of poetic qualities, of the limitations of idyllic form and figurative language, are topics that offer to students already trained and mature, rich rewards for careful and extended study, but they suggest the preparation of the instructor, or the analytical study of the critic, and lie wholly outside of the field of work possible for those at a distance from libraries, and without the personal guidance of some competent scholar. What, then, is the ordinary reader to do? Is it possible for him to gain any true understanding, however inadequate, of these noble poems?

On first consideration, the task seems difficult to the point of absurdity, but we should remember that for a generation thousands of persons without special training, and but moderately gifted, have read and enjoyed Tennyson's Idylls. It is also true that the greatest poets and artists have always appealed directly to their fellowmen of the common sort. Let us seek in *Idylls of the King* the basis of this appeal, and find thus, if we may, some suggestion for guidance. The complexity which renders the Idylls difficult furnishes also a wider range of selection for purposes of reading or study than other literature gives. In more than one of the Idylls, Tennyson follows so closely a mediæval tale that the reading of the poem merely as a modern version of the older story richly repays the student. The weeks devoted to this study will not be misspent if no more than this is done; every library should contain editions of Malory's *Morte Darthur*, the best modern versions of the Arthurian romances, and a translation of the beautiful Welsh stories of the Mabinogion. In these books, readers have in hand the sources of Tennyson's Idylls. The stories of themselves have a perennial interest, and in them students will learn how, from some shadowy, early reality, the heroes of chivalry have acquired vitality and permanence as literary characters and have been used, over and again, to express the ideals of many generations. Incidentally, the pupil comes to understand, also, the source and use of literary material, and is thus the better ready for direct study of this difficult topic when, in later years, he comes to it. In one, at least, of the required Idylls, the allegorical passages approach in definite symbolism the form of the fable, and are well adapted for literal and methodical interpretation by readers not prepared to follow Tennyson's more subtle suggestions of spiritual meaning.

But the reading of the Idylls merely as versions of the adventures related by Malory seems superficial, and unworthy of the noble character of the series in which they stand. Each Idyll contains a part of the larger story of the king, beginning with the coming of Arthur and ending only when he rode from Almesbury to that great "battle in the west" where he died. Surely it were a pity for students to read these poems and fail to find in them the ideal knight for the portrayal of whom all were written. But it is in passing from the separate story to the larger meaning running through successive Idylls that the task of interpretation becomes difficult. The deeper meaning of the story of Arthur's life, of his noble purpose thwarted through the sin of the queen, of the broken fellowship of knights gone to "follow wandering fires," is scantily indicated and the topic, moreover, requires maturity and acumen.

There is, probably, no literature in which narrative structure, pure and simple, is more complex and difficult than in *Idylls of the King*. Students who have had careful training in æsthetics and in the theory of the drama are often unable to disentangle the mingling threads of plot. Each Idyll has its own form and structure, but the characters of the larger drama take their parts in its scenes, and incidents of slight import in the story often receive an undue emphasis because of the part they play in the development of the action running through the series. Moreover, as the series progresses, with the nicest artistic sense of proportion, Tennyson calls attention, less and less, to the separate story, and mingles in increasing ratio characters and scenes purely of the main action. All this can be followed appreciatively only after considerable study of literary form, especially in the drama and in fiction. The clue to follow in the unfolding of this great drama must be sought in the earliest phase of Tennyson's conception and in the first Idyll of the series. The poet was a boy, himself, when King Arthur won his allegiance, and the devotion rendered to his ideal knight in those early years never died out of his heart. We must bring back the hero-king whose figure is to run through all the Idylls as connecting link, giving to each a meaning wider than its own story bears. Malory's *Morte Darthur* in the original text is easily read, and references to selected chapters corresponding with Tennyson's stories are given for each Idyll. If possible, attention should be given, first, to Arthur, as he appears in tradition, and in the old stories of the middle ages. The material is abundant and interesting. The wall map, even, may be called into service; the definite location in England of the places around which traditions of Arthur still linger will give a reality to the old Celtic stories not to be gained in any other way.

But it is in "The Coming of Arthur" that the figure of the king, who with his "secret word" and his Table Round is to be a part of every Idyll to follow, stands forth. In this Idyll, it is related how Arthur "made a kingdom and reigned." The description of Cameliard, overrun by heathen hordes, is a picture, in small, of Arthur's own kingdom, Britain. His task was the bringing of safety and order into every part of his realm. For success in this purpose, he must be recognized as Uther's son and crowned as king. After this, he himself believed that his greatest aids would be a queen, one with him in purpose, and a fellowship of brave knights sworn to do his will. As the story goes on, Merlin had Arthur crowned, and after, he wedded Leodogran's daughter and established the famous "Order of his Table Round." All is summarized in the glorious song, "Blow trumpet, for the world is white with May." The Idyll closes with proof of the strength of the crowned, wedded king, whose knights "were, for a space, of one will with himself."

If the reader has little notion of the meaning of the secret word, or of vows so straight that those who took them "were pale as at the passing of a ghost," he will readily conceive of The Round Table as a fellowship of knights bound by the most sacred vows to uphold the king. In succeeding Idylls, each knight belongs to this fellowship, or seeks admission, and the honor and success of life is, for him, bound up in his worthiness as a member of Arthur's Table Round. In each separate Idyll, the king forms so slight a part of the narrative that without the aid of the Table Round and the relation of each knight, through this fellowship, to the king, Arthur's name and character will scarcely linger in the memory. But when in succeeding Idylls, knights as different as Gareth, Gawain, and Lancelot, each worship the king, and fear his disapproval, the strength of the fellowship as an order becomes a real thing to the student. Through it, the shadowy king, always in the background, is nevertheless unforgetable; and his character, revealed, by little and little, in the ideals of conduct required of his knights, is illumined and remains in the memory like the vision of some beautiful face seen in early years and then withdrawn.

In the deeper meaning of this Idyll, |in the purpose of the king, is found the master key of the great and noble tragedy to follow. From the joyous beginning of a time, the action moves on, scene by scene, to days of doubt and suspicion; then, through base rumors and acts more base, until evil days draw on, of jealousy and false piety, in which, ere the end, the goodliest fellowship of the world was broken up. Each purpose of the king, each aid on which he leaned, failed to fulfill his hope, and in the growing certainty of this failure the action moves forward to the moment of climax, and of catastrophe, in which we see the king bereft of his knights, betrayed by wife and friend, alone, in utmost need. As, in the beginning, the heart of his purpose was the secret word, so, in the end, it was his doom that he saw all the purpose of his life spoiled, his realm "reeling back into the beast."

This, then, is the clue to follow in the study of the narrative structure of *Idylls of the King*. Each separate Idyll fulfills an essential part in the central purpose, and the story told in it must be understood in the light of the greater drama moving forward through the series. The story of the changes and additions through which part was adjusted to part and each Idyll related with artistic nicety to all that went before or followed, need not be repeated, but every one who reads or studies these poems should bear in mind the successive phases of poetic imagination and purpose through which they grew. It was a peculiarity of Tennyson's genius that a beautiful thought, or phrase, or fancy, once in the possession of his mind, was a treasure beyond price. A conception which had moved him deeply could never be wholly given up; it lingered in his imagination after the plan of which it had formed an essential part was abandoned, and subtly modified and enriched later conceptions. The central thought of the poet in his final arrangement of *Idylls of the King* was infinitely richer and greater than his early conception, yet the figure of the "blameless king," moving among his knights . . . "as the conscience of a saint among his warring senses," . . . "the highest and most human, too," bears a haunting suggestion of the epic hero, and Merlin now and again fills a part which might well be borrowed from the earlier plan.

Indeed, it would seem that every phase and form of meaning

ever harbored in Tennyson's mind may be traced in some part of these richly varied poems. The poet cherished, in a long life, a conception which drew into itself the fullness, the strength and beauty of his own soul, ripening slowly as years brought maturity, experience, and freedom. To this is due the manifold, inwrought beauty of the Idylls, richer and more subtly complex than any other English verse. If many theories of interpretation have arisen it is because for each some correspondence may be traced here or there in the Idylls. To those who would have had him say, in age, whether his meaning lay in this interpretation, or in that, the poet replied that for each, the truth must lie in his own understanding of what he had read and in the fervor of spiritual perception kindled within him. As his own mind traveled backward along the way it had come and rested with pleasure on each earlier phase of its growth, so he seemed to feel that in his writings might be found something corresponding to each.

"And truth is this to me and that to thee;
And truth, or clothed, or naked, let it be."

Appreciation of these wonderful poems is only to be gained in a manner comparable, in some degree, with the slow process of their growth. Through long and intimate study of each part, through tracing each thread of meaning subtly interwoven, an intimate understanding of the poet's thought comes to the attentive mind, a higher and finer kind of vision; in the midst of rich detail s revealed the greatness of the design, and the beauty and wealth of poetic suggestion hidden in the verse are seen as the expression and adornment of deeper meanings, each lying within the other, as spirit hides in an outward form.

The *Idylls of the King* are rich in literary and poetic beauty, in phrases that linger in the memory, in expressions of rare and significant charm, or in lines pregnant with meaning, "The myriad cricket of the mead;" . . . "rapt by all the sweet and sudden passion of youth toward greatness in its elders;" .
"Obedience, . the courtesy due to kings," and many more. Tennyson is here, as every where, infinitely complex, and his verse

is a composite in which beautiful descriptions, phrases rich in poetic significance, mingle with intangible qualities that, like an atmosphere, pervade and give color to all. The finest intelligence is taxed to follow the working of the master's mind, and perhaps only persons rarely endowed with poetic insight catch the full significance and beauty of each part of these wonderful poems. This is not the place for consideration of those subtle and carefully selected means of literary art employed by the poet in the expression of his purpose, but whatever phase of rythmic quality or poetic beauty is selected for attention, it proves as complex, as wonderfully wrought of many elements, as nicely adapted to the inner meaning, as is the larger plan, of which it forms a part. Whereever we spend most careful and loving study, however small the picture, or slight the incident, there we find that the prevision of the poet still surpasses our appreciation, and it is the highest of tributes to Tennyson's breadth and power that he never permits us, while the mind dwells upon beautiful detail, complete in itself, to forget the higher use it is designed to serve. In the music of the verse, in the vision called up in the mind, we catch his meaning, as one may see in the sensitive lineaments of some human face, now and again, in transient glimpses, the quick, sentient spirit, the very flame of life itself, more beautiful than the features it illumines.

Here and there, in the study of *Idylls of the King* to follow, are topics intended to suggest systematic study of the rich literary art in these poems. When the time at command is limited, these topics may easily be omitted, but those who have felt, even faintly and from afar, the touch of creative impulse, will linger longest here, and find in this phase of study richest reward. The poetborn has no need of aid or suggestion in reading the poems of another, but many of us halt along the way, and must avail ourselves of every means of enkindling our more feeble imagination if we are to attain, at length, the joy of insight and the vision of complex and wonderful beauty such as filled the mind of the author of *Idylls of the King*.*

*This introduction is in part quoted from essays by the writer, printed elsewhere.

DIRECTIONS FOR NOTE-BOOK WORK.

All note-books should be paged, and running titles, in abbreviated form, should always be placed at the top of each page. Careful attention should be paid to the grouping of facts and to the subordination of particulars to the more general statements of which they are divisions or illustrations. Generous white space should be left between groups of particulars that the form of arrangement on the page may emphasize the group as a separate division.

Whenever the particulars entered in the note-book are to be used as evidence in proof of statements, or when conclusions will be based upon them, exact references to books cited as authorities should be given. Without the authority and a presentation of exact data, the statements in note-books have no value which should be accepted either in discussions, or in recitation. The principle that note-books should contain only data really valuable for reference, arranged and indexed in such form as to be accessible without loss of time, should be adhered to.

When a subject of study such as Idylls of the King gives rise to several distinct note-book topics, these may easily be kept in one book by the device of page references, placed at the foot of the full page, to the continuation of the topic farther over in the book; the corresponding reference to the page from which the topic is continued must also be placed at the top of the new page.

In note-book work, it is a mistake to write full sentences or paragraphs. The note-book should be a graphic, organized summary of the reading or study of the pupils, and should be packed full of exact, well-arranged data likely to slip from the memory without this aid. The purpose of note-book work is not the making of a substitute for the books from which the items have been gathered. It should, instead, be a key, an *index rerum*, which will guide the student without loss of time to the items he needs, or the paragraphs he has found valuable. By the aid of a well-kept note-book the student should find it possible to review the important part of a dozen books in as short a time as the careful first-reading of one of them required. References to pictures, maps, or references pertaining to the subject, etc., may be placed in the margin of the page of the note-book, or on alternate blank pages left for this purpose. The references to Malory's *Morte Darthur* placed at the head of the Topics for Study for each Idyll illustrate this subject. They have been taken from the note-book of the editor, and in the copy of the *Morte Darthur* used, the passages referred to are so marked in the margin of the page that the eye finds them instantly.

It is not intended that each student should include all the note-book topics in his study. The preliminary topics should be prepared and placed in the note-book for reference, in the beginning. Each one should arrange *Plot Outlines* in convenient form for reference and comparison. This is of special importance in the study of "Idylls of the King," on account of the complex relation of the plots; each Idyll should be compared with the older tales from which the story is drawn as a study in selection; and the dramatic development of the cycle must be distinguished from the plots of the separate episodes in which it mingles. Definitions and analyses should also be placed in the note-book for illustration and reference. Other topics may be chosen or omitted according to time and personal inclination. *The Study of the Idylls of the King* is arranged with special reference to the cultivation of critical acumen. Insight, the power that discerns literary qualities and defines by analysis and comparison degrees of excellence, or ideals of the poet's art, may be acquired only by such work as the student of science does in the laboratory. For this reason, each reader should give special attention to one or more of the topics designed to aid him in the formation of intelligent and critical opinions about the Idylls and the qualities of Tennyson's verse.

NOTE-BOOK TOPICS FOR STUDENTS.

Preliminary:
  I. For reference: A list of the Idylls of the King, in the order in which they were written.
  II. A list of the Idylls of the King, showing the groups in which they were successively published.
  III. A chronology of Tennyson's life showing the time of composition and of publication of the Idylls of the King.

For Study of the Idylls:
  IV. List of Characters in each Idyll.
  V. List of Characters common to several Idylls, or to the series.
  VI. Plot Outlines:
  a. Of the story of the separate Idyll, showing the beginning of the story, the essential steps of its development, its climax, and conclusion.
  b. Outline showing the cycle story in the story of the Idyll; that is, if the Idyll is one act in the drama of the cycle, show the plot of the act, and how it advances the story of the series.

NOTE.— Those events or facts belong in a plot outline which *determine* subsequent events. They give the effective presentation of the theme and lead inevitably to the climax, and conclusion. It is necessary, always, to distinguish carefully between such events or facts as have determining force, and those incidents which are illustrative, or contribute to character building.

The plot structure of *Idylls of the King* is peculiarly complicated. Each Idyll has its own subject and plan of dramatic presentation. In each, certain characters, situations, conditions, contribute to the development of the general plan running through the series. In each Idyll, there must, therefore, be a subject which is the central artistic conception, and an arrangement of plot for the presentation of this theme; there is, also, in each, a subject which is the expression of a distinct purpose, or step, in the larger plan of the series. The separate Idyll in relation to the series is, in a manner, similar to the scene in the act, or to the act in the drama. It follows that the same incident may be of dramatic importance in the series and merely incidental in the Idyll, or the reverse. Plot outlines should, therefore, be arranged to show, in parallel, this double significance; the plot elements of the Idyll may be noted in sequence, with indication of beginning, climax, conclusion, and those belonging to the series may be repeated in their own arrangement, according to importance. Many fine critical distinctions must be made in studying the relation of these complex plots, and, in the result, the reader will gain an appreciation not to be arrived at in any other way, of the poet's artistic skill in narration.

VII. Character Studies:
These are not similar to the character studies of fiction or the drama, but have, rather, an artistic quality, a nicety of adaptation to an ethical purpose.

VIII. Quotations:
Select only such quotations as are complete when severed from the context, and of great value for beauty of sentiment, accuracy of analysis, or clear statement of profound truth. Seek to find a few choice passages, rather than to make many quotations.

NOTE-BOOK TOPICS FOR CRITICAL STUDY.
(FOR ADVANCED AND SPECIAL STUDENTS.)

IX. List of characters drawn from Malory, or other sources, and adapted. Analyses of means of adaptation, etc., with references, should furnish material, in the end, for a critical study.

X. Old characters markedly changed in presentation, with notes of reasons, and references.

XI. In the plot, critical notes of incidents, characters which have different value, relation, or use, in the Idyll and in the series.

d. For each, use and relation, both in Idyll and in cycle must be noted. There is no better means of studying the complicated relations of mingling plots.

XII. In the use of old material:
- *a.* Perversions, or changes of characters.
- *b.* New interpretations of old incidents.
- *c.* Invention on the part of the author.
- *d.* The literary end served in each instance noted under 'a,' 'b,' 'c.'

XIII. The allegorical element in *Idylls of the King*:

XII. and XIII. are special topics for those interested. The notes should show how idealism modified the author's plan, and indicate in a trustworthy manner the literary use made of the allegorical element. With this aid, the reader may consider the critical question whether Tennyson distinctly intended to thread his narrative with an allegorical element in subordination to his main purpose, or halted between two opinions, inclining, at different periods, to one or the other.

XIV. Evidence that Tennyson changed or modified his general purpose in the series. This topic should be discussed only at the close of the series, in connection with the consideration of the epic or idyllic form of the poem, the allegorical interpretation, etc.

XV. References to literature having close connection with Tennyson's verse giving a different expression to the same purpose, useful for comparison in critical study, or as illustrations of figures of speech, etc.

XVI. Tests, analyses, and definitions:

Used in the study of poetic qualities, dramatic power, etc.
This topic is designed for the few who are making a special study of literary art.

XVII. Characteristics of Tennyson, the poet.

These should be notes of qualities of verse, artistic or idyllic setting, use of figures of speech, habit in description, means employed to gain results, etc. They should furnish material for a critical discussion of the artistic qualities in Tennyson's verse, or in his narrative.

XVIII. Idealism in Tennyson.

XIX. Special Topics.

College students and students of literary art will find special topics for themselves in the study of Tennyson's versification, or of the idyllic qualities of the poem, or in other similar subjects. The note-book for these topics is simply a means of collecting and organizing data for the formation of opinion; the material may then be used in presenting the subject in an intelligible and interesting written form.

THE USE OF THE TEXT.

It is desirable to use a copy of the text not too valuable for marking. It is often convenient to note a series of facts by marginal references, or by words, such as "Theme," "Plot," etc., and it facilitates later study of the characters to write the initial letter of the name of each important character in the margin whenever any description, analysis, or other indication of personality occurs. It will then be possible to trace characters through the narrative without re-reading.—*From " The Study of Romola."*

THE READING OF CRITICISM.

Many of the essays that have been written in interpretation of Tennyson's Idylls are full of insight, but the reading of criticism should be deferred until the conclusion of this study. The mind, like a mirror of clear glass, is easily clouded; knowledge of the opinions of others, held in esteem, often casts a shadow that obscures, past recognition, the original activity of the intelligence. The reading of criticisms upon literature of which one is ignorant is much like reading a guide-book in place of visiting a foreign land. When students have become thoroughly familiar with the Idylls and, through them, with certain qualities and characteristics of their author, critical opinions will serve their true purpose, that of suggesting to one student the conclusions of another with which he may compare his own.

WRITTEN PAPERS IN STUDY CLUBS.

It is not intended that the topics for study in this guide shall be distributed to different members of study-clubs, or assigned for written papers. All members of the study club should read, study, and make notes for each meeting upon the same topics. In this way only, is it possible to secure keen interest or intelligent discussion and criticism. It is also essential, if a well proportioned view of the year's study is to result, that each one should regularly do a minimum amount of work in common with all. The college instructor would never think of assigning one topic only of a long, cumulative series for individual study and presentation, as a means of obtaining a satisfactory knowledge of the whole subject, and the device is as inadequate in the study club — usually less homogeneus in natural ability and training than the college class.

If written papers are considered an essential feature of the club program they may be arranged, (a) on outside topics, frankly miscellaneous, or of current interest, while the main part of the time is reserved for discussion of topics of study under the guidance of a presiding member ; or, (b) these papers may be on topics closely connected with the subject of study, but not essential parts of it ; or, (c) an afternoon, once in several months may be set aside for written papers with the distinct understanding that a certain number of most important topics already canvassed in study and discussions shall be presented in written form. This is the most important and valuable kind of written work for the study club, for it is original, that is, based upon individual study of the literature ; it presents the results of study mingled with personal opinion slowly matured, and it offers for the enjoyment of all a contribution in literary form of the best that each one can do. For the individual, also, the effort of composition and presentation furnishes a test of the permanent results gained from the months of study, and is an index of personal power and independence,— for the one who leans heavily on others must bring an incoherent series of observations, while the real student presents opinions which have survived criticism and discussion.

WRITTEN WORK FOR ADVANCED STUDENTS.

In this study of "Idylls of the King" are included certain topics intended to suggest critical study of the most careful and accurate kind. This study involves comparison, analysis, distinction of subtle artistic elements, and, finally, critical opinion arising from individual study of literary art. The expression of critical opinion in accurate analyses, with subtly drawn distinctions, is perhaps the severest test of acumen, and of resource in the art of expression that can be found. This part of the study offers training in laboratory methods of criticism and in the art of critical writing; for this reason, all definitions, distinctions, and conclusions should be written in the choicest and most accurate diction at the command of the student. Topics for this kind of study are found in the analysis and interpretation of the literary art which is the subject of study, and at every opportunity the student should express the results of study, or his own conclusions in critical paragraphs, or in short essays. Any critical question which involves comparison, analysis, or synthesis, and the formation of opinion, or the definition and illustration of artistic qualities, or purpose, will serve as theme, and the effort of giving adequate expression to impressions in the mind will require the keenest exercise of critical ability, and the most patient revision of phrase or word to secure the expression that is most fit. These topics are designed for college and advanced students, and especially for students of literary art who seek aid in acquiring broad culture and in the discipline through which would-be-writers gain freedom and skill in the expression, in literary composition, of their own thought.

References for Study of Idylls of the King.

BOOKS WHICH SHOULD BE OWNED.

The Idylls of the King, edited by W. J. Rolfe, is a convenient handbook.
Essays on Tennyson's Idylls of the King, by Harold Littledale.
Le Morte Darthur, by Malory. The Globe edition, The Macmillan Company, is uniform with "The Works of Tennyson."
The Study of Idylls of the King, full series, by H. A. Davidson.
A complete edition of Tennyson's poetry, containing the latest revision. Either the Globe edition, The Macmillan Company, or The Cambridge edition, Houghton, Mifflin and Company, is satisfactory.

A Life of Tennyson, either,

a. Tennyson, by Sir Alfred Lyall, English Men of Letters; or
b. Alfred, Lord Tennyson, A Memoir, by his son. (May be had in one volume. Where possible, this Memoir should be owned instead of the smaller life.)

BOOKS FOR THE LIBRARY.

Tennyson's Life:

Alfred, Lord Tennyson, A Memoir, by his son.
Alfred, Lord Tennyson, by W. E. Wace.
Alfred, Lord Tennyson, by Arthur Waugh.
Tennyson, Poet, Philosopher, and Idealist, by J. C. Walter. Scribner's.
Tennyson, by Sir Alfred Lyall, English Men of Letters. The Macmillan Company.
Alfred Tennyson, by Andrew Lang. Modern English Writers.
The Poems of A. H. Hallam, by R. Le Gallienne; Remains in Verse and Prose, A. H. Hallam. J. Murray.
Memories of the Tennysons, illustrated. By Rev. H. L. Rawnsley. The Macmillan Company.

Homes and Haunts of Tennyson, by G. G. Napier. Maclehose and Sons.

Records of Tennyson, Browning, and Ruskin, by Anne Thackeray Ritchie.

The Study of Idylls of the King (full series), by H. A. Davidson. The Study-Guide Series.

Older Literature used as sources of Arthurian story:

Le Morte Darthur, by Malory, edited by Sir E. Strachey; Globe edition.

Six Old English Chronicles, containing Nennius's "History of the Britons," Geoffrey of Monmouth's "British History, etc.;" Bohn's Libraries.

Arthur and the Table Round, chiefly after the French of Chretien de Troyes, by W. W. Newell, 2 vols.

For Henry Morley's discussion of Arthurian Romance, in "English Writers," see vol. iii., chapter vi.

"Romances of Arthur and of Antiquity," chapter iv., in "Short History of French Literature," by George Saintsbury.

The Mabinogion, translated by Lady Henry Guest, cloth, 50 cents. The Macmillan Company.

The High History of the Holy Grail, translated by Sebastian Evans, Temple Classics.

Morte Arthure: re-edited for students by Mary McL. Banks. Longmans, Green & Co.

Reading for Young People:

Stories of the Days of King Arthur, by G. H. Hanson, London. T. Nelson & Sons.

Legends of King Arthur, by F. Warne. An abridgment of Malory's Le Morte Darthur.

Stories from the Wagner Operas, by H. A. Guerber.

Popular Romances of the Middle Ages, by G. W. Cox.

Wonder Tales from Wagner, by A. A. Chapin. Harpers.

The Story of the Rhine Gold, by A. A. Chapin.

Wotan, Siegfried, and Brunnehild, by A. A. Chapin.
The Fall of the Nibelungs, translated by Margaret Armour.
The Court of King Arthur, by W. H. Frost. Scribner's.
A Garden of Romance, edited by E. Rhys. New Amsterdam Book Company.

Criticism and Interpretation:
Poetry of Tennyson, by Henry Van Dyke.
Tennyson, His Art in Relation to Modern Life, by S. A. Brooke.
Poets and Problems, Part II., by G. W. Cooke.
Essays on Lord Tennyson's Idylls of the King, by Harold Littledale. The Macmillan Company. Especially valuable for the explanation of terms, references, etc.
A Study of the Works of Alfred, Lord Tennyson, by E. C. Tainsh. The Macmillan Company.
Victorian Poets, Chapters v. and vi., by E. C. Stedman. Chapter vi. contains a careful study of Tennyson's indebtedness to Theocritus.
Thoughts about Art, by Philip Gilbert Hamerton; chapter v contains a valuable discussion of Tennyson's skill in description.
Studies in the Idylls, by Henry Ellsdale.
Illustrations of Tennyson, by J. C. Collins.
Abbey's pictures of the Quest of the Grail. For a small, illustrated catalogue of these pictures, write to Curtis and Cameron, Pierce Building, Boston, Mass.
Classical Echoes in Tennyson, by W. P. Mustard. The Macmillan Company.
Handbook of Tennyson's Works, by Morton Luce.
In "Poems by Tennyson," edited by Henry Van Dyke and D. L. Chambers, The Athenæum Press,—Introduction, III., Tennyson's Use of his Sources; IV., Tennyson's Revision of his Text; VI., The Qualities of Tennyson's Poetry; and, in the Appendix, the Study of Tennyson's metres.

The Geography of Arthur and the Historical Arthur:
King Arthur in Cornwall, by W. Howship Dickinson. Longmans, Green & Co.

Merlin, or the Early History of King Arthur, by H. B. Wheatley. Early English Text Society. The introduction by J. Stuart Glennie, "The Old Arthur Land," and "Note," containing the opinions of the historian, C. H. Pearson.
Introduction to the Globe edition of *Le Morte Darthur*.
English Histories and Encyclopædia Britannica.
For Tennyson's interest in the geography of Arthur's Land see Memoir I., 274, 322, 415-16, 460-3.

BOOKS FOR ADVANCED AND CRITICAL STUDY.

Older Literature used as Sources, Texts, etc.;

Le Morte Darthur, by Malory, edited by Dr. H. Oskar Sommer, published by David Nutt, London. An expensive and exhaustive edition, in 3 vols. Vol. iii., Studies on the Sources.

The Mabinogion, translated and edited by Lady Charlotte Guest, published by Bernard Quaritch.

The Legend of Sir Gawain, by Jessie L. Weston.

The Legend of Sir Lancelot du Lac, by Jessie L. Weston. Published in London, by David Nutt.

Arthurian Romances unrepresented in Malory's "Morte d'Arthur," No. II. Tristan and Iseult. Rendered into English by Jessie L. Weston. New Amsterdam Book Co.

Sir Gawayne and the Green Knight, edited by Richard Morris, Early English Text Society. For the character of *Gawain*, see preface, and also *The Flourishing of Romance*, pp. 114-15; and English Writers, iii., 279, vi., 59, 240.

Studies in the Arthurian Legend, by John Rhys, The Clarendon Press, for Celtic sources and traditions.

Morte Arthure, edited by Edmund Brock. Early English Text Society. This volume contains the text of Sir F. Madden's "Syr Gawayne," published in the list of books of the Bannatyne Club.

The Inflexions and Syntax of the Morte D'Arthur of Sir Thomas Malory. A study of fifteenth century English, by Charles Sears Baldwin. Ginn and Company.

Popular Studies in Mythology, Romance and Folklore, vol. i., Celtic and Mediaeval Romance, by A. Nutt.
Theocritus, Bion, and Moschus, Translation and Essay, by A. Lang The Macmillan Company.
Tennyson's Idylls of the King and Arthurian Story, from the XVI. Century, by M. W. Maccallum.
The Classical Heritage of the Middle Ages, by Henry Osborn Taylor. The Columbia University Press.
The Flourishing of Romance, chapter iii., by G. Saintsbury. Scribners.

Variations in Tennyson's text:

The Growth of the Idylls of the King, by Richard Jones. J. B. Lippincott Company.
Variations in Merlin and Vivien. The Dial, May 10, 1901.

The Epic and the Idyll:

Short Studies in Literature, by Hamilton Mabie, the Epic, 148-52; Some mediaeval Epics, p. 153—
Early English Literature, by B. Ten Brink. The Hero Saga, the Epic, book i., chapters ii., iii.
Lectures on Shakespeare, by B. Ten Brink. In Lecture iii. is a distinction between dramatic and epic qualities.
Introduction to the Iliad and The Odyssey, by R. C. Jebb.
A History of Classical Greek Literature, chapters i., ii., iii., by J. P. Mahaffy.
Hegel's Aesthetics, Part ii., chapter viii., edited by J. S. Kedney.
Introduction to Criticism on Paradise Lost, edited by Albert S. Cook.
Aristotle's Theory of Poetry and Fine Art, with a critical text and Translation of the Poetics, by S. H. Butcher. Second edition, 1898, Macmillan. Discussion of the Epic, pp. 280—
The Epic and Romance, by W. P. Ker.
The Classical Heritage of the Middle Ages, by Henry Osborn Taylor. The Columbia University Press.

Victorean Poets, by A. C. Stedman, chapters v. and vi., Tennyson's Indebtedness to Theocritus.

The Beginnings of Poetry, by F. B. Gummere. The Macmillan Company.

The Flourishing of Romance, chapters, ii., iii., iv., by Saintsbury. Scribners.

English Writers, by Henry Morley, vol. iii., p. 279—; vol. vi., p. 59—, p. 240—

Contemporary Criticism:

Four Idylls of the King: The Spectator, p. 125, July, 1859. A discussion of Idyllic qualities and form.

The Epic of Arthur, Edinburgh Review, April 1870. A discussion of the dramatic purpose and unity of the series.

The Arthurian Legends in Tennyson, Contemporary Review, vol. iii., p. 501.

Correspondent—The meaning of the Holy Grail, The Spectator, May 10, 1873.

The Dramatization of the Arthurian story, The Dial, p. 160, Mar. 16, 1896, and p. 197, April 1, 1896.

For the allegory in the Poems, see The Contemporary Review, January, 1870, (by Dean Alford); The Contemporary Review, May, 1873; The Spectator, January, 1870 (by R. H. Hutton).

Topics for Study.

PRELIMINARY.

The Poet.

I. How was Tennyson educated previous to going to the university?
   (1) Years in school.
   (2) Home study, years, teachers, subjects.
   (3) What did he read?

NOTE.—A list of books, by years, with the age of the reader indicated, will throw light on the habit and development of his mind.

(4) What did Tennyson teach himself in these years at home?

(5) How did he learn to write?

NOTE.—A statement of the writing attempted by the lad, showing subjects, amount, etc., may be made. It is instructive to compare the results with the amount and kind of composition written by high school pupils now, but a generalization as to Tennyson's genius or precocity would be misleading without an inquiry in regard to other young persons of that generation.

II. How long a time did Tennyson spend at the university? In what subjects was his regular work?

III. What reading or study outside of his regular work did Tennyson do at the university?

IV. Who were Tennyson's intimate friends when he was at the university?

What common interest brought these young men together? In what common pursuits did they find companionship?

What permanent results of value accrued to Tennyson from these friendships?

The composition of Idylls of the King:

V. When did Tennyson's interest in the idyllic form of verse begin? What early models did he study?

VI. What Idylls did Tennyson write, beside *Idylls of the King?* Which were earliest? Make a list of Tennyson's Idylls in the note-book, with dates of composition or publication.

VII. When did Tennyson first contemplate the writing of a poem on the subject of King Arthur? What, in outline, was the earliest form of his conception?

VIII. Make in the note-book a list of all the Idylls in the series, showing:

(1) The time and order of composition.

(2) The time of publication.
(3) The Idylls published in one group, in various editions.
(4) The final order of arrangement. Indicate the Idylls that were added after the general plan and arrangement had been determined.

The Epic:
IX. Define the essential characteristics of the Epic in this manner: First, write a definition or explanation of what you understand by epic form, from the impression existing in your own mind. This definition must be so expressed that it will include the great epics with which you are familiar. Secondly, consult dictionaries and discussions of poetic form; make an outline of essential characteristics according to authorities; compare with your own, and test by your own knowledge of some epic. For references, see bibliography.

The Idyll:
X. Define the Idyll in the same manner as the Epic, and consider,
   (1) Characteristics essential to the Idyll.
   (2) Limitations of the Idyllic manner.

TENNYSON'S ADAPTATION OF THE IDYLL TO ENGLISH THEMES.

Early Attempts:
XI. (1) When and how did Tennyson become interested in the Idylls of Theocritus?
   (2) What poems represent his first attempts to write an Idyll?

Œnone:
XII. For indebtedness to Theocritus, see Stedman's *Victorian Poets*, chapter vi.
XIII. (1) What is the theme of Œnone?
   (2) What is the outline or plan by which this theme is developed?

(3) Is this plan dependent upon the idyllic setting for effect?

(4) Why is the narrative in the form of retrospect?

The Lotus Eaters:

XIV. For indebtedness to Theocritus, see above. For a different literary treatment of the same theme, see Lowell's "The Mariners," and Matthew Arnold's "The New Sirens."

(1) What is the theme of "The Lotus Eaters?"

(2) What is the outline or plan by which this theme is developed?

(3) Is the Idyllic setting essential to the presentation of the theme? Show in detail reasons for your opinion.

Ulysses:

XV. (1) Show, as above, theme, outline, or plan of presentation, idyllic setting.

(2) Stedman says that this poem embodies the Homeric idea of a hero. What were the characteristics of the Homeric hero? In what lies the special skill of Tennyson's presentation?

The Lady of Shalott:

XVI. (1) Show, as above, theme, outline, or plan of presentation, idyllic setting.

The Palace of Art. As above.

XVII. This poem is especially suitable for the study of Tennyson's liking for allegorical meanings.

XVIII. (1) In which of the above poems is there a second theme, allegorical, or ethical, in meaning?

(2) Is the allegorical meaning secondary and subordinate, or of chief importance?

XIX. How do you define the difference between the allegorical and the ethical, in these poems? Illustrate each from the poems.

The Coming of Arthur.

The Old Story:

1. Arthur's birth; *Le Morte Darthur*, book i., chapters i., ii., iii.
   Arthur's marriage; book iii., chapters i., ii.
   Excalibur; book i., chapter xxiii.
   The Round Table; book iii., chapters i., ii., iii., iv., xv.
      book iv., chapters iv., v.

The Historical Arthur:

2. *a.* From what historical personages have traditions of Arthur probably been derived?
   b. What facts, if any, have been accepted as historical?
   c. Possible dates.

NOTE.— Consult especially the *Encyclopædia Britannica*, the editor's preface to *Six Old English Chronicles*, and to *Le Morte Darthur*, Ten Brink's discussion of the growth of the Hero Saga, and English Histories. It is not intended that readers shall make an investigation of the historical question with a view to arriving at a conclusion in regard to the facts of Arthur's existence and life. It is desirable, rather, to gain an understanding of the sources of the old traditions, and histories, of the manner of their growth and the literary habit, in the middle ages, of intermingling fact, tradition, and legend, in one narrative.

The Geography of Arthur:

3. (1) Locations assigned to Camelot.
   (2) Location assigned to Glastonbury, Joyous Gard, Tintagil, Avalon, Lyonesse.

NOTE.— Special references on this subject will be found in the bibliography. It is one that has attracted some attention, especially among Celtic scholars. The reader must remember that many discussions are no more than special pleas devoted to showing the plausibility of certain theories. The real significance of the question in literature is found in its relation to the origin and transmission of the Arthurian traditions, but the topic belongs rather in the field of mediæval, or comparative literature.

The Coming of Arthur:

4. Where was the land of Cameliard?
5. About how long after the Romans left Britain is the historical Arthur supposed to have lived?
6. Who were the heathen who troubled Leodogran? Where did they come from?

NOTE.— Use a map of England showing the military roads built by the Romans, the wall built to keep out the Picts, etc., and notice the situation of Leodogran's kingdom. No exact geography should be attempted, but these lands of the poet's imagination have a certain indefinite correspondence with the map of ancient Britain, just as the story of Arthur's wars and adventures is drawn from the chronicles of the early historians. Tennyson himself spent considerable time in the parts of England where tradition locates Arthur and his shadowy city of Camelot.

7. What is the purpose of the description of the land of Cameliard in the beginning of "The Coming of Arthur?"
8. What is the real subject, or theme, of "The Coming of Arthur?"
9. Where is the beginning of the dramatic action, or plot, of this Idyll? What proves it?
10. What was the most important incident in the coming of Arthur to aid Leodogran? Why?
11. *a.* In lines 1-60, what facts or incidents antecedent to the beginning of the story are told?
    b. For each, show what in the beginning of the plot would fail of full significance without the mention of antecedent facts, and in what way this artistic necessity is met.
12. What was the immediate result of Arthur's visit to Leodogran's kingdom?
13. Two events of great importance in the narrative of the Idylls occurred between the return of Arthur from Cameliard

and the sending of his knights to ask for Leodogran's daughter,— what were they?

The Stories of Arthur's Birth:

14. *a.* What stories of Arthur's birth are given?
    b. Where did Tennyson find each?

Tennyson's Use of these Stories:

15. *a.* What is the literary, or artistic excuse for the introduction of these stories in the narrative of "The Coming of Arthur?"
    b. Why was Leodogran dissatisfied with the stories of Arthur's birth told by the Knights?

NOTE.— This is the story told by Malory and he had it from Geoffrey of Monmouth and other historians of Britain; it was long supposed to be literally true.

16. What three things in the story of Queen Bellicent were most important? Why? Did she answer Leodogran's question?
17. What was the meaning of the story which the queen had from Bleys?
18. What did Merlin's answer to Bellicent mean?
19. What is the meaning of Leodogran's dream? Did it influence his decision? Explain your understanding of how he made up his mind.
20. Summarize all the facts given about Arthur from his birth to the time of his marriage. Which of these did Tennyson especially emphasize?
21. In what particulars did Tennyson change the order of the events of Arthur's life? Why?
22. *a.* What was Malory's story of how Arthur came by Excalibur?
    b. What allegorical interpretations of Excalibur as a symbol have been given?

NOTE.— The numerous Celtic interpretations may be found in "Studies in the Arthurian Legend," by John Rhys. Many of these are fanciful. The most interesting symbolic use of Excalibur, and of the scabbard is that in *King Arthur* as played by Sir Henry Irving.

"Greet the dawn, the night is o'er,
England's sword is in the sea."

23. Where was Arthur married? What was Tennyson's reason for choosing a place, which does not again appear in the Idylls, for the ceremony?

NOTE.—The poem "Lancelot and Queen Guinevere" is Tennyson's full version of lines 449-51. It should be read here; what was Tennyson's reason for reducing this part of the story, in the Idyll, to a mere reference?

24. Malory's story of the marriage of Arthur is given in book iii., chapters i. and ii.

    a. How has Tennyson changed the story? Why?

    b. The most significant thing in Malory's story Tennyson has omitted,—why?

25. Make an outline showing all the steps in the plot from the beginning to the end of the dramatic action of the Idyll.
26. In what do you find the climax?
27. In what lies the conclusion?

"The Coming of Arthur" in the Cycle:

28. What passages of the coming of Arthur are not essential parts of the real subject and the plot of the Idyll as a separate story?

If you regard the series of Idylls as a dramatic action, each idyll in the series fulfills a definite purpose in relation to the whole; as, in the drama, the act is complete in itself but is a part of the play and holds a carefully adjusted relation to other acts before and after. In a series in which each idyll has a complete and independent plot of its own the relation of the idyll to the dramatic action running through all is loose, and, often, the plots intermingling, are intricate, since incidents of importance in the idyll may signify little in the cycle; or, on the contrary, passages which in the idyll are mere description, may be of first importance in the cycle.

29. How do you define the purpose in the cycle, of "The Coming of Arthur?"
30. Which characters in "The Coming of Arthur," are essential to the dramatic action of the cycle? The discussion of this point must be based on "The Coming of Arthur" only, if it is to lead to a critical estimate of whether Tennyson clearly indicated, in the beginning, the characters that he intended to use.
31. What plot elements belonging to the cycle are found in "The Coming of Arthur?"
32. There is a certain unity in the arrangement of those elements in the Idyll, belonging to the larger dramatic whole, as in the single act of a drama. In relation to this unity:
    a. Where is the beginning?
    b. Where do you place climax and conclusion?
33. Show in relation to the theme and plot of each, why the conclusion of "The Coming of Arthur" as a separate Idyll must be different from the conclusion of "The Coming of Arthur" as a part of the cycle.
34. What conditions were essential, in Arthur's mind, for making a kingdom and reigning?
    How do you define the "secret word" and Arthur's purpose?
35. Was this purpose understood by his knights? By the queen?
36. What evidence on this point do you find in the text?
37. Certain situations have a different value in the cycle plot from the one they hold in the idyll. For each of the following, show what the meaning, or value, is, (*a*) in the cycle; (*b*) i the Idyll, with the critical reason for each.
    a. The description of the land of Cameliard.
    b. The stories of Arthur's birth.
    c. Merlin's word.
    d. Bellicent's description of Arthur's crowning.
    e. The pledge between Arthur and Lancelot.
    f. Dubric's charge.
    g. The song.
38. At the close of "The Coming of Arthur:"

a. What were the king's plans and purposes?
b. On what agencies did he chiefly rely for carrying out his plans?
c. From what sources was disaffection most likely to arise?
d. Had Arthur enemies, or friends whom he could not trust?

NOTE.—The question, here, is one of Tennyson's artistic skill in the beginning of his great plot; the preparation for what is to follow must be sought here, and we must ask what possibilities of success or failure lie enfolded within the outlines of the narrative set down in the Idyll. No part of Malory's story, or of the development in later idylls, is relevant to the discussion here called for.

GARETH AND LYNETTE.

The Old Story:

Le Morte Darthur, book vii., chapters i.-vi., xiv.-xvii., xix., xxi., xxxiv.-v.

The Round Table, book iii., chapters i., ii., iv. Book iv., chapters iv., v.

The name of the knight in Malory's tale is Sir Beaumains.

Topics for Study:

1. What is Malory's story of the origin of the Round Table, and of how it came into the possession of King Arthur?
2. How did Tennyson change this story? Why?
3. How many seats were about the Round Table? How were vacancies filled? On what conditions?
4. What were the conditions of knighthood in the middle ages? Upon what in the old conception of knighthood did Tennyson seize for his purpose?
5. What is the relation of the Round Table to Arthur's purpose in the Idylls?
6. When Gareth came to Camelot how many seats had been filled?
7. What, in outline, is Malory's story of Sir Beaumains?

NOTE.— This outline should be made, either by marking Malory's text, or in the note-book, for the purpose of referring in the study of the Idyll, to characters, incidents, etc., taken from *Morte Darthur*.

8. In the cycle plot, there are two reasons for beginning this Idyll in a place far from Arthur's court and kingdom,—what are they?*

NOTE.— For Tennyson's first location of Arthur's mystical city, Camelot, see Memoir ii., 122. Later, he became familiar with traditions which localize Arthur in many places in Wales and in England, south of the Thames; the location which seems to have been in the poet's mind in the Idylls, apparently, was not so far west as Lyonesse. The truth seems to be that the historical Arthur, according to the custom of kings, in those days, moved from place to place with his followers and all his court. He often made a long stay where he halted, hearing and deciding questions which, now, would go to some small court of justice, and otherwise setting in order the wild populations of his kingdom. In this way, certain locations came to be recognized as halting places for the King on his journeys, and, for each one, local tradition handed down in names, stories, and antiquities, the deeds of Arthur and his knights, while those who told the tale believed that here, indeed, was the city of the King. These traditions probably all originated in some real connection with Arthur, now impossible to trace.

9. What is the real subject, or theme, of "Gareth and Lynette?"
10. In what is the beginning of the plot, or narrative, of this Idyll?
11. What is the chief element of pathos in the incidents of Gareth and his mother?
12. What were the ideals of life in Camelot at the time when Gareth came? Do you detect any jarring note?

* Topics for Study on the Idylls required for college entrance, in "*The Study of Four Idylls of the King*," The Study-Guide Series, may be used to supplement those given here.

13. Has the keystone of Camelot any meaning with reference to the Idylls? †
14. What is the interpretation of the lines beginning, "For an ye heard a music, like enow?" P. 322, Globe edition.

NOTE.— Compare with the references to music in "Palace of Art," "Amphion," "Œnone," and Wordsworth's "Power of Sound." See also Gayley's Classic Myths, for the building of the walls of Troy and of Thebes to music.

In the presence of the King:

15. What is the significance of the impression made on the youth, Gareth, by the King?
16. When Gareth came forward one of the knights saw that he was in disguise,— by what marks did he discover his gentle birth and breeding?
17. Did Tennyson find the characteristics attributed to Sir Kay in *Morte Darthur?*
18. For what purpose in this Idyll, does he use the character of Sir Kay?
19. For what reason was each one of the three judgments pronounced by the king selected by Tennyson for use here?
20. Tennyson's story of how queen Bellicent sent secretly to court is different from Malory's; What reason for the change do you find in the plan of this Idyll?
21. In Malory's narrative, who knighted Gareth? In Tennyson's, who? Why was this change made? Find the reason in the artistic requirements of the plot.
22. *a.* Who, in Malory's story, was Linet?
    b. What reasons from a literary point of view had Tennyson for developing this character?
23. Where did Gareth get his motto? What is the reason, in the Idyll, for emphasizing this motto?
24. Make a plot outline of the quest of Gareth from the moment

† See Littledale's "Essays on Idylls of the King," p. 87.

of his setting forth to the moment in which the object of the quest is achieved.

25. In this outline, trace the changing relation of Lynette and Gareth, showing how each step was won.
26. The Song fulfils more than one purpose in the Idyll:
    a. Trace its relation with the plot.
    b. Show in how many ways it is an artistic expression of subtle and pervasive elements of Tennyson's purpose.
27. What is the significance of each one of Gareth's conflicts in the Idyll? In the allegory?
28. How do you interpret the Cave, the Morning Star, etc? For what purpose are they introduced here?

NOTE.— Littledale discusses the sources from which Tennyson borrowed his allegory in his essay on this Idyll.

29. What is the importance of the quest of Gareth in the full plot outline of this Idyll?
30. Where is the climax of the dramatic action of the Idyll?
31. Where is the conclusion?
32. Which ending do you consider the truer art, that of Malory, or that of Tennyson? Find your reasons in the nature of the story told by each.

Gareth and Lynette in the Cycle:

33. Which characters in "Gareth and Lynette" belong to the cycle?
34. What elements of dramatic importance in the cycle are found in this Idyll?

NOTE.— An outline should be used to show the cycle plot mingling with the story; or, if an outline or plot analysis has been made for the Idyll, all parts significant in the cycle may be starred or underlined. The relative significance of incidents or characters in the story, and in the cycle, should be noted, as in "The Coming of Arthur."

35. What is the "situation" of the dramatic action in the cycle at the close of "Gareth and Lynette"?

36. Compare the ideals of Arthur, the king, with those of his knights, as illustrated in this Idyll.
37. What little threads of plot from "The coming of Arthur" are repeated in this Idyll which seem to point forward;—that is, which seem a preparation for future developments? Give references for each, to lines in both Idylls.
38. Trace the allegory mingling with the narrative from the beginning of this Idyll. Show, in each part, how it serves to express Tennyson's purpose. Is the allegorical element most significant in the Idyll, or in the Cycle?
39. What was Tennyson's purpose in placing Gareth and Lynette second in the series of the Idylls?
40. Why was Malory's Sir Beaumains well suited to Tennyson's purpose?

Critical Comparison of Tennyson's Idyll with Malory's text:

41. *a.* In *Morte Darthur*, book VIII., mark in the text an outline of the adventures of Sir Beaumains.
    b. Note in the margin all incidents, etc., used in Tennyson's Idyll.
42. Using the above outline for the purpose of comparison, show in detail, how Tennyson adapted Malory's story to his own purpose, and gave it the significance he wished. Inquire especially,
    a. In what he changed or developed characters introduced.
    b. To what incidents he gave new meanings.
    c. Which characters, incidents, or situations in Gareth and Lynette are of Tennyson's own invention? Does his reason for these lie in the Idyll, or in the relation of the Idyll to the Cycle?
    d. For what phrases, descriptions, etc., was Tennyson indebted to Malory?
    e. Present in writing your own estimate and opinion of "Gareth and Lynette," especially with reference to Tennyson's indebtedness to Malory's *Morte Darthur*.

43. Explain the literary reason for retaining in an Idyll written especially with reference to the series, so marked and fantastic an allegory as the one that threads this narrative.

44. Select three or four passages that you think finest in Gareth and Lynette. Inquire, in the case of each, why you selected the lines: — was it for the thought, or the sentiment? For the beauty of expression? For imaginative qualities? For what reason? What tests did you use in coming to a decision?

Which do you think the nobler poem, "The Coming of Arthur," or " Gareth and Lynette "? In the comparison, inquire in regard to,

a. Poetic qualities and idyllic setting.
b. Dramatic or epic qualities.
c. Power of imagination shown.
d. Nobility of sentiment and style.

What *idyllic* passages, or pictures, do you find in " Gareth and Lynette?" In what is the idyllic setting essential to full expression of the meaning in the passages chosen?

GERAINT AND ENID. PART I.

The Old Story:

Tennyson found the material for this Idyll in the Mabinogion, in the translation of Lady Charlotte Guest, the first edition of which had been published in 1838. For variations in the incidents and the arrangement, see Littledale's essay, and compare Idyll and translation. This translation makes accessible to the ordinary reader one of the most beautiful of the mediaeval tales. It is less diffuse and remote in interest than many of the old romances, and the reading will richly reward the student who appreciates literary qualities, classic simplicity, and beauty in the narrative. For the correct pronunciation of Enid, see Memoir, II., p. 125.

The composition of this Idyll was begun in the spring of 1856; in July and August of that year, Tennyson, with his wife and children, visited Wales. He halted at Caerleon-on-Usk, and visited many places in which traditions of the old Arthurian stories have been handed down; among others, Cardiff Castle, the seat of the Sparrow-Hawk in the tale, and later, for six-and-twenty years, the prison of Robert, Duke of Normandy. Here, in the midst of the scenes of this beautiful story, the poet finished the composition of it, and more than one description is a literal transcription from nature by this supreme artist in words, of what he saw, and of the impressions that moved him. While in Wales, both Tennyson and his wife studied with local school masters that they might read and pronounce the original Welsh. It was after this that he changed the line, "Had wedded Enid"... to adapt it to the Welsh pronunciation of the name.

In mediaeval times, there were continental versions of this tale, but it is generally conceded that it was really of Welsh origin.

Topics for Study:

1. Make an outline of the dramatic action of the story of Geraint in the Mabinogion showing:

    a. The beginning.
    b. The plot in outline.
    c. The climax.
    d. The conclusion.
    e. The theme.
    f. The relation or value of each incident in the advancement of the action.

2. After writing which Idyll did Tennyson begin "Geraint and Enid"? For what purpose was the poem written?
3. When were the "Marriage of Geraint" and "Geraint and Enid" first published? Under what titles?
4. When was the tale divided into two parts? Why?

NOTE.— The reason for the place of the division, in the poem and criticism of it, are necessarily deferred until after the discussion of the plot outline.

5. If the two tales are really one episode in *Idylls of The King*, make, for use in the following topics, a plot outline of the two Idylls showing ;

   a. Beginning of action.   c. Climax.
   b. Steps of development.   d. Conclusion.

6. What is the theme of these idylls, as a separate incident ? In what is the beginning of the plot ? How do you prove it ?

7. Why was the point of division placed where it is ? Show from the artistic structure of this story whether either part has a separate unity ; whether the incidents admit of division in any but the mechanical sense ; if so, whether division at this point can be justified artistically or not.

8. How is the antecedent material introduced and treated in these tales ? What peculiarity, in this respect, do you find? What is the reason for it?

9. Note each point where the narrative halts and returns to past events ; in the discussion, show (*a*) the necessity in the plot for the antecedent material ; (*b*) the excuse for its introduction ; (*c*) the place and the manner of resuming the main narrative.

10. Compare the plot outline of the story of Geraint in the Mabinogion with the plot outline of Tennyson's Idyll, and inquire,

    a. How Tennyson has changed the order and arrangement of the story.
    b. How he has varied characters, incidents, etc.
    c. What additions, if any, he has made.
    d. For what details of description, phrase, etc. was he indebted to the Mabinogion ?

11. For each item, the author's reason with reference to his plan, or his meaning, in the Idyll, is the important point for consideration. This is note-book work; the particulars, with references, should be collected and arranged for use as evidence in the discussion.

12. In the "Marriage of Geraint," trace from the beginning, in the character of Geraint, every suggestion that points toward the "shadow of distrust" which, later, he harbored.
13. How was this suspicion planted in his mind? Show whether it was wholly wrought out of Geraint's own mind, or whether it was fostered and grew by outside influence.

In Part Two, "Geraint and Enid;"

14. Enid's disobediences,— what was the cause and the effect of each?
15. How was Geraint convinced of his own error?
16. Why did Geraint fear to meet the King?
17. What was the test of Geraint's restored faith in Enid?
18. In what is the moment of climax in this story of "Geraint and Enid?"
19. In what is the conclusion?
20. In what was Geraint's task in Cornwall similar to Arthur's in his kingdom? In what was it different?

In the Cycle:

21. For what purpose was the story of Enid and Geraint first written?
22. There is in this Idyll both a double parallel and a double contrast: discuss and illustrate each from the Idyll.
23. What characters and what plot elements belonging to the series of the Idylls do you find in the two parts of the story of Geraint and Enid?
24. Through which characters is this Idyll brought into relation with the plot of the series, and what important step in the development of the dramatic action of the series is in "Geraint and Enid?"
25. Is the plot of "Geraint and Enid" really subordinate to its use in the development of the larger drama of the series?
26. Do you find anything in the incidents, the characters, the sentiments, which are in the spirit of a civilization later than that of the original story?

27. Do you find in the story of this Idyll qualities belonging to the old romantic tale, but not consistent with the modifications introduced by Tennyson to adapt it to his own purpose?

NOTE.— This should be note-book work, with tests carefully chosen, or should be omitted. It is not intended in this topic to open the way for a discussion which shall be no more than the expression of opinion. Real criticism must be based upon the most careful and original work on the text, and the discussion should be directed to the interpretation of the poet's purpose, and his selection and artistic adaptation of means to the end in view.

28. Do you find an allegorical meaning in the tale of Geraint, or in any part of it? What was Tennyson's attitude toward the allegorical interpretation of the Idylls?

Critical Comparison of Tennyson's Idyll with the story of Geraint the Son of Erbin:

This comparison must be omitted by students who have not a translation of the Mabinogion. An inexpensive edition of the translation is now published; see p. 19.

29. Make an outline showing the arrangement of all important incidents in the original story:
30. Where did the story open? What incident was the beginning of the plot?
31. In the original story, what was the source of Geraint's spleen?
32. How, in the old story, did Earl Yniol lose his estate?
33. How long a time was occupied by Geraint's quest, in the original story?
34. What is the most important difference between the Idyll and the original story in the impression made on the reader? In the inferences to be drawn from incidents?
35. Criticize the original story, as a story, in point of subject matter, interest, structure, characters, narrative art, literary qualities.

NOTE.— Each one of these topics may be made the subject of special study and the conclusions may be presented and illustrated in written papers.

36. Arrange parallel outlines of the story of "Geraint, the Son of Ebin," and of Tennyson's "Geraint and Enid," with spaces in each, for additions, or omissions.

a. Using this arrangement for reference, show Tennyson's selection and omission of incidents for his own use, noting especially, omissions, condensations, etc.

b. Show Tennyson's rearrangement in the order or sequence of incidents, in order to make a plot which should express his own purpose, or theme.

NOTE.— Tennyson's purpose must first be defined; then his beginning, with the reason for it, should be discussed. After this, the steps of the plot, with the introduction of antecedent material and the reason for it,— to the climax, and the conclusion.

c. Note and discuss, giving reasons, changes in incidents used, and additions made by the poet.

d. Note, with illustrations, Tennyson's indebtedness, throughout his Idyll, to the older story, in literary qualities, phrases, descriptions, etc.

GERAINT AND ENID. PART II.

The Idylls of the cycle first composed are more Homeric in quality than those of Tennyson's later time. There is in them the truth, simplicity, and dignity of the Greek epic. The reader is moved with delight in the story pure and simple. He feels a certain fidelity to tradition in the narrative, for all the subtlety of spiritual meaning gradually unfolded, and sees the noble dignity of heroic times woven like a spell around common deeds. Similitude in two pieces of literature lies chiefly in the spirit that, like an atmosphere, pervades the whole. The clear perception of a quality so delicate and elusive as kinship in literature may be gained only from intimate knowledge of the type, and of that which resembles it. The similitude may be a superficial one of phrase or idiom, or it may mark a correspondence in atmosphere and deeper meaning. The following suggestions for the comparison of the qualities called Homeric in these Idylls with the Illiad or the Odyssey, are intended to furnish, for those unfamiliar with Greek literature even in translation, a means of gaining a practical impression of the characteristics of these epics. There has been no attempt to make the study exhaustive, but if the reader is able to limit and define the impressions gained they will have a certain critical value and serve for comparison. The points chosen for attention were arrived at by noticing and classifying, in "Geraint and Enid," such expressions and illustrations as could, with fairness, be said to give a Homeric quality, or tone, to the poem.

The reader should own: *The Illiad of Homer*, done into English prose by Lang, Leaf and Myers; *The Odyssey of Homer*, by G. H. Palmer; *Theocritus, Bion, Moschus*, rendered into English prose by A. Lang.

37. Read as extensively as possible in the Iliad and the Odyssey, in one or more books of each; mark for reference:
    a. Figures of speech.
    b. Hyphened adjectives.
    c. Descriptions, especially of persons or acts.
    d. Emphasis placed upon physical qualities, or beauty of person.
    e. Descriptive phrases of especial beauty or fitness.
38. Mark throughout the Idylls, "The Marriage of Geraint," and "Geraint and Enid," all passages which seem Homeric. Notice especially:
    a. The peculiarity of classical figures of speech.
    b. The use of hyphened adjectives.
    c. The objective and simple character of descriptions.
    d. The epic character of the narrative, the story for its own sake.
    e. The dignity given to commonplace acts and the effect; as, "the sweat of their great labor."
    f. The frank admiration of physical qualities and beauty of person.

g. Descriptive phrases of special beauty or fitness.

h. Note and illustrate such qualities in Tennyson's poem as seem suggestive of characteristics of the Homeric narrative, distinguished from narratives in later times.

Figures of Speech in Geraint and Enid:

39. What do you understand by the Imagination? Describe and illustrate the activity of your own mind which you suppose to be the Imagination.
40. Describe and illustrate the activity of your own mind which you call Fancy.
41. In what lies the essential difference between these two?
42. Illustrate from familiar poetry both Imagnation and Fancy.

NOTE.— Avoid definitions found in dictionaries and rhetorics. Without reading and thought, the interpretation of definitions is often narrow and misleading. The references given below are to discussions that will stimulate thought and that indicate the relation of the imagination to creative production. Attention to the activity of his own mind is the reader's true source of knowledge on this subject.

References:

For discussions of Imagination and Fancy see,

Coleridge's *Lectures on Shakespeare*, Bohn's ed., pp. 74, 220.

Coleridge's *Principles of Criticism*, edited by A. J. George, in chapter iii.

Hegel's *Æsthetics*, edited by J. S. Kedney, Part I., chapter viii.

Wordsworth's *Prefaces to the Lyrical Ballads*, edited by A. J. George.

Ruskin's *Modern Painters*, Part II., chapters i.-iii.

See also Wordsworth's Essay, "Of Poetry as Observation and Description," (Prose Writings).

43. In your own mind, wherein lies the pleasure of a figure of speech?

44. Which gives you greater pleasure, an extended figure like the simile, or condensed figures, figurative and suggestive language, etc ? Illustrate.
45. In figures of speech, what are the conditions that secure beauty and perfection ?
46. In these idylls, mark all figures of speech. In regard to each inquire :
   a. The purpose of the figure, that is, what it illustrates?
   b. In what the beauty lies.
   c. Is the implied comparison defective, or incompletely suggested ?
   d. What is the effect of the figure upon the mind?
   e. Is the figure subordinate to its use in the text, so that it does not form a digression, or divert the thought from the idea it should illustrate ?
   f. Select three figures that seem to you most perfect. What tests do you use in determining?
   g. Select three figures that seem to you most beautiful. What tests do you use ?
   h. Select three figures that seem to you best to fulfill the purpose for which each is introduced.
   i. Which figure of speech in each of these Idylls seems to combine all these qualities in the highest degree ?

NOTE.— If there is time for it, a study of poetic qualities in verse may be introduced here. It should include imagination, vision, vowel harmonies, and elements of beauty, not technical. The discussion of vowel harmonies in Swinburne's verse, found in *Victorian Poets*, by E. C. Stedman, will be helpful for comparison. The essay of R. L. Stevenson, "On Some Technical Elements of Style in Literature," distinguishes between prose rythm, and poetic rythm.

BALIN AND BALAN. PART I.

1. The Old Story: *Le Morte Darthur*, book ii. For the "Dolorous Stroke," chapter viii. For Tennyson's prose version, Memoir, vol. ii., p. 134.

Topics for Study:

2. When was "Balin and Balan" written? For what purpose?
3. Why was it placed between "Geraint and Enid," and "Merlin and Vivien" in the cycle? See Memoir.

NOTE.— An outline of incidents prepared so that the parts used by Tennyson may be indicated, is very useful.

4. How did Tennyson change the significance of the tale? By what means?
5. At what period of Arthur's life did the adventure of "Balin and Balan" occur? How did Balin get his sword?
6. In *Le Morte Darthur*, what became of his sword after Balin's death?
7. What is the significance of the title, "The Dolorous Stroke," in Tennyson's prose version?
8. What is the real subject of the story of Balin and Balan in *Le Morte Darthur?*
9. What parts of Malory's narrative did Tennyson omit? Why?
10. What did Tennyson add to the story found in *Le Morte Darthur?* Did he change the significance of any of the incidents?
11. Make an outline of the dramatic action of the Idyll, "Balin and Balan."
12. In what lies the beginning of the action?
13. How early in the Idyll is the theme suggested? What is it?
14. Where is the climax? How do you prove this?
15. Wherein is the conclusion?
16. Show whether these incidents are really a part of the plot of the Idyll and subject to its development :
    a. The conversation in the queen's bower.

    b. The visit to Pellam's court.
    c. The taking of the spear.
    d. Vivien's song.

17. What elements of noble tragedy do you find in this dramatic action?
18. Which do you think the more perfectly developed tragedy, Tennyson's story, or Malory's? Why?
19. Why did Tennyson choose that Balan's chief aid in overcoming his violences should be the thought of the queen?
20. How many rumors of the queen's infidelity came to Balin? What was the origin of each?
21. Why did he believe Vivien's story? Why did Balan disbelieve it?
22. Why did Tennyson wish Balin to die believing the queen innocent?

NOTE.— In this Idyll, again, evil rumor arises concerning the queen; again, the truth of the rumor is not admitted, while its force is lessened by Guinevere's lofty character and the ideals of life in the court over which she presided. But although Balan, the pure, died believing in the purity of the queen, in some subtle way Tennyson deepens the shadow of mistrust first breathed upon her fair name in the preceding Idyll; the force of the rumor lies in the possibility of its truth, in the foreboding that sinks deep in the heart of the reader.

BALIN AND BALAN. PART II.

In the Cycle:

23. What is the theme of "Balin and Balan" in the cycle?
24. What plot elements belonging to the cycle are found in "Balin and Balan?"

NOTE. — This Idyll, written last, and with the purpose of making the transition from the time of Gareth and of Geraint to the evil days of Merlin and Vivien less abrupt, must have been planned with the full conception of the cycle in mind, and should, therefore, be studied with especial care in relation to the meaning and the arrangement in the full series. In this Idyll, the subject of "Balin and Balan," as a separate story, coincides most nearly with the purpose fullfilled by it in the series; the emphasis, however, differs. In the Idyll it is upon the individual, Balin; in the cycle, upon the incipient demoralization of the court and the influences which wrought confusion in the mind of the unhappy knight.

25. What was Tennyson's theory of Lancelot's early devotion to the queen?
26. What change in the relation of these two is indicated in this Idyll? Was Lancelot or the queen responsible for this change?
27. What was Lancelot's meaning in, "Fain would I be loyal to the queen," and in, "Lo, these her emblems drew mine eyes away?"
See also Tennyson's poem, "Sir Lancelot and Queen Guinevere."
28. Did the author intend the reader to interpret the rumors that came to Balin as evidence of the queen's guilt?
29. What is the relation, in the plot, or in the artistic background, of the incident and the rumors about the queen and Lancelot, to the story of "Balin and Balan?" To the plot of the cycle?
30. How do you explain, "Man's word is God in Man," in connection with the king's "Secret word," and the line, "The old order changeth yielding place to new," in the "Coming of Arthur?"
31. How did Arthur test Balin on his return?"
32. How is Arthur's definition of ideal knighthood broadened in this Idyll?"
33. What were the characteristics of King Pellam's religion?
34. What points of difference from Arthur's religion are emphasized?
35. What was Arthur's comment upon Pellam's piety?
36. What was Tennyson's purpose in representing King Pellam's religion, "adopted in a rival heat," as a kind of parallel to Arthur's?

37. What is the significance of King Pellam and of the holy spear in the dramatic development of the cycle?
38. Why is the Idyll of "Balin and Balan" the proper place for the introduction of this element in the plot?
39. What difficulties in the accomplishment of Arthur's purpose are shown in this Idyll?
40. What secret dangers threatening the Table Round and the permanence of Arthur's ideal are shown in this Idyll?
41. In the allegorical meaning of the Idyll, what do the following represent:
   a. Balin, and his name, "Le Savage?"
   b. Balin's difficulties in court life?
   c. The Demon said to live in the wood?
   d. Balin's brother Balan?
   e. Vivien?
42. a. What theory of life is represented in Vivien's song?
   b. Why should this theory of life have had especial force in the middle ages? See the note at the close of topics on this Idyll.

Literary qualities:

43. Which do you consider the finest lines in "Balin and Balan?" Why?
44. Which do you consider the finest narrative or descriptive passage in this Idyll? Why?

NOTE.— In selecting passages, such tests of excellence as have already been determined should be applied. In no instance should selection be made merely on account of liking or of approval of the sentiment. Critical acumen is to be developed only through recognition of those qualities that determine the inclination of the mind.

45. How many extended figures of speech do you find in "Balin and Balan?" Repeat for this Idyll the study of figures of speech and figurative language outlined for "Geraint and Enid."

discusses for
of Merlin in
of Robert
accedent story
an had been
and thus, from
g all things
ower of fore-
d the secret
him to build

NOTE.— In the middle ages, two theories of life swayed the minds of men. The one was ascetic in nature and taught that enjoyment and pleasure are but self-indulgence. Religious devotees denied themselves the use of all things that appeal to the senses or minister, even indirectly, to bodily appetites and passions; they interpreted loving "father and mother more than me" in the narrowest sense and turned away from all human ties. On the other hand, men of full vitality and independent nature, oftentimes turned from doctrines so repugnant to all natural instincts, and asserted the conviction that tastes and passions are but the expression of human nature, with the inference that whatever ministers to them must, therefore, be right. This position was violently condemned as the source of all evil, and many, in passionate protest against this judgment, carried indulgence to excess and justified themselves. The mediæval romances of Parzival and of Tristan represent, typically, these two theories of life, and in "Balin and Balan" asceticism and the opposing philosophy of life are sharply contrasted. The one finds typical expression in King Pellam and his religion; the other pulsates in Vivien's song, which expresses belief in the right of the individual to enjoy all good things as his natural inheritance. Light, air, the bounty of nature, youth, beauty,— all are, and to these correspond natural appetites and passions; these are, therefore, good, and man has been made that he may live in the light of the sun. In "Rationalism in Europe," Mr. Lecky discusses the relation of asceticism and of the contrasting theory of life to the development of man.

MERLIN AND VIVIEN.

The Old Story:

Merlin and Nimue ; *Le Morte Darthur*, book iv., chapters i., iv. King Arthur and the Table Round (Newell), vol. ii., p. 134.

Merlin's birth; Nennius's History of the Britons, § 39-42, p. 400— printed in *Six Old English Chronicles*, Bohn's Libraries.

Geoffrey's British History, book vi., chapters xvii., xviii., in *Six Old English Chronicles*.

For variations in the text of Merlin and Vivien see:

The Growth of The Idylls of the King, by Richard Jones, chapter ii., 4 and 5; The Dial, May 16, 1901, p. 327.

For the meaning of unusual words, references, etc., see Littledale's essay on "Merlin and Vivien." For the source of the natural scenery in Merlin and Vivien see Memoir, I., 114.

NOTE.— The stories of Merlin's birth furnish a remarkable illustration of the way in which legends or traditions change, develop, and gather new material, as they pass through the hands of successive narrators. The story told by Nennius is brief, definite, literal; Geoffrey adds many details. Malory, whose narrative has the charm of literary grace, refers more than once to Merlin's birth. These narratives are easily accessible and afford the material for a bit of literary study that will illustrate the vitality and variability of old stories when used as literary material. The story of Merlin's agency in the hasty marriage of Uther Pendragon and the guardianship of Arthur are even better for the same purpose, since, in this instance, Malory repeats the story of older writers with little change except in the literary form of the narrative. Compare Geoffrey's British History, book vi., chapters xvii.-xx. and *Le Morte Darthur*, book i., chapters i.-iii.

Dr. Sohmer in his great edition of *Morte Darthur* discusses for scholars the sources of Malory's work. The story of Merlin in chapters i-vii., of book i., he condensed from the *Merlin* of Robert de Borron. Dr. Sohmer summarizes also a long antecedent story from the same source in which it is related that Merlin had been begotten by a fiend who ensnared a holy woman, and thus, from his father, the fiend, had the power of understanding all things past, and from his mother, the holy woman, the power of foreknowing the future. In this story, also, Merlin revealed 'the secret of the two tables' to Uther Pendragon and persuaded him to build a round table with one vacant seat.

Topics for Study:

1. *a.* Read "Merlin and Vivien," omitting the lines from the 6th, "For he that always bare,"— to the 142nd, "The wily Vivien stole from Arthur's court."
    b. Read the omitted lines after having read the tale of Merlin and Vivien to the end. These lines and a few other short passages were added to the poem in 1874; in what way do they change the significance of the whole? That is, what was the theme or purpose of the poem as first written? What is the theme or purpose of the poem as it now stands?
2. What would be the true title of "Merlin and Vivien" as a separate episode?
3. Make a plot outline of the Idyll, "Merlin and Vivien," marking the beginning, climax, and conclusion of the dramatic presentation.
4. What part is antecedent to the beginning of the Idyll?
5. What are the reasons, from a literary point of view, for introducing these steps in the plot as antecedent material rather than in the form of direct narrative?
6. What was Vivien's motive in following Merlin?
7. What was Merlin's ambition? What was the cause of the deep melancholy that drove him from court?
8. In what words of Merlin, if in any, do you find a double meaning? Explain the meaning of the words in Merlin's understanding of them. To fulfill what purpose did Tennyson give them double meaning?
9. To what weakness of character did Vivien appeal in her efforts to overcome Merlin?
10. In what is the climax of her attempt?
11. What emotions did Tennyson portray in "Merlin and Vivien?" Trace and note in sequence the different phases of emotion described in this Idyll, as you would trace the development of a plot.
12. With what feelings do the emotional elements of "Merlin and Vivien" affect the reader?

13. In the allegorical interpretations of the Idylls, for what does Merlin stand? What is the significance of his death?
14. What do you understand Tennyson's interpretation of the allegorical meaning to have been?
15. What was Malory's story of Merlin's death? Notice also the story of the enchantment of Merlin used by Arnold in "Tristram and Iseult?"
16. Who was Nimue in Malory's tale? What was her character?
17. What incidents and what characters in "Merlin and Vivien" are taken from the *Le Morte Darthur?* What has Tennyson added or changed? In each instance, for what reason?

NOTE.— The reasons for changes or additions must be found in the conditions necessary for the development of the dramatic purpose, or in the æsthetic relation of literary and poetic qualities to the central purpose of the author. The topic should be studied analytically with the aid of the note-book. The critical questions involved can be discussed with profit only on the basis of exact knowledge of the texts of Tennyson and of Malory.

18. How did Tennyson secure the atmosphere, or setting, in the sense of tone-color, that he creates in this Idyll? What was his object in it?

In the Cycle:

19. What is the true subject of "Merlin and Vivien" as a part of the cycle?
20. What plot elements of the cycle are found in "Merlin and Vivien?"
21. What is the relation of the death of Merlin to King Arthur's purpose? To the queen?
22. Select in "Merlin and Vivien" four descriptions which seem to you most beautiful; in the case of each ask:
    a. In what lies the beauty?
    b. How is the description related to the narrative, and to the main purpose of the Idyll?

The Queen's Error:

23. Trace from the beginning of the cycle the steps by which the queen's error has been brought before the reader.
    a. "In the Coming of Arthur."
    b. "In Gareth and Lynette."   d. "In Balin and Balan."
    c. "In Geraint and Enid."   e. "In Merlin and Vivien."

Questions:

24. At the close of "Merlin and Vivien," has any real error of the queen been brought to light?
25. At the time of Merlin's death, what changes had taken place in Arthur's court since his crowning? To what causes were these changes due?

The distinction between Idyll and idyllic:

"Vision" may be described as a little picture created at once, having a certain unity, or organization of detail. This little picture may be incidental to the narrative and serve to adorn it harmoniously, or it may be so intimately a part of the incidents that the figures and acts of the story mingle with the natural setting and both together compose perfect pictures which are essential in the narrative itself. It happens, sometimes, also, that a corresponding sequence and unity in the phenomena of nature accompanies the development of the poetic narrative. When this occurs there is, inevitably, a certain dramatic element in the mere setting of the picture, in the descriptive passages, which, as the story proceeds, tend toward an emotional climax. The perfect artist in poetry so mingles the two elements that moments of great dramatic interest in the narrative coincide with manifestations of nature which seem an expression of the emotion of the action and at the same time increase the intensity of it. The field within which this sort of composition is possible is a very narrow one, for if undue emphasis is given the natural setting it ceases to be subordinate to the central figures of the narrative, and we have the pastoral in which the human element forms no more vital part than other features that compose the scene; while, if the interest in the action mingling with the scene be intense and the issue involve deeply the welfare of the actors, our sympathies are stirred until we forget the setting and await, breathless, the decision of fate; but this is no longer the Idyll; we are moved by the pity and finality and sorrow of noble tragedy. In this difference in the relation, or proportion, of elements in the narrative and the description, lies the distinction between the Idyll as a literary form, or type, and that idyllic quality characteristic of certain kinds of verse, or even of prose. The Idylls, "Merlin and Vivien," and "Lancelot and Elaine," invite, more than others of the series, study with reference to critical definition of the distinction between the Idyll as a literary type and those idyllic beauties that so appropriately adorn many varieties of composition. Preliminary study of "Merlin and Vivien" for this purpose is suggested in the topics given below. For a continuation of this discussion see page 63, in the study of "Lancelot and Elaine."

Idyll, or Idyllic

 a. Make an outline of those scenes in "Merlin and Vivien" which are a setting of the action.
 b. Make an outline showing the dramatic elements of transition, change, etc., in natural phenomena which accompany the incidents of the story.
 c. Show from these outlines and from the poem the use made of the setting and phenomena of nature to excite, or to accentuate emotion, or to create atmosphere.
 d. Trace the successive phases of nature used as setting for the narrative, through the poem, to show whether they have an arrangement and unity of their own.
 e. Show at what critical times action and phenomena of nature are so intertwined as to be inseparable.
 f. Is the action, or plot, at any time determined by natural phenomena?

NOTE.—This is necessarily note-book work, but the outlines should be merely memoranda, showing exhaustively, and in sequence, every illustration in this Idyll falling under the topic, and when completed should serve as the basis of critical discussion, which may be either oral, in class, or written.

LANCELOT AND ELAINE.

The Old Story:

Le Morte Darthur, book xviii., chapters viii.-xx.

NOTE.—In Malory's narrative, four Elaines are mentioned; Elaine, King Ban's wife, mother of Sir Lancelot, named Galahad Lancelot; Elaine, wife of Nentres, king of Garlot; Elaine, daughter of King Pelles, and mother of Galahad, son of Lancelot; Elaine le Blank, of Astolat.

The story of Lancelot and Elaine begins with a picture and the statement of a fact; after this the poet goes back to the very beginning of his tale:

1. Make an outline of the story from the beginning to where Tennyson resumes the narrative of Lancelot and Elaine, in line 397.
2. In the antecedent material, lines 28-397, what is the peculiarity of the arrangement? Show graphically, by outline, or diagram, the dependence of each new antecedent, and in the discussion consider;
   a. The point of introduction.
   b. The reason for it in the artistic plan of the Idyll.
   c. The literary devices used as excuse for it, and what marks the end of it.
3. In this antecedent material, what parts of it belong in the larger story of the cycle?
4. In what is the beginning of the plot of this Idyll? What proves this?
5. There are in this Idyll several stories intermingled; the outlines of each are so clear that from the poem a narrative sequence may be arranged for more than one of them.
   a. In Elaine's story, in what was the real beginning?
   b. In the story of Lancelot, as told in this Idyll, where was the real beginning?
   c. In the story of the Queen's jealousy, in what was the beginning?

6. The description of Lancelot's entertainment in Astolat may be treated as a short story and compared with the story of the entertainment of Geraint by Earl Yniol and his daughter.
   a. Outline this story from the coming of Lancelot to his departure.
   b. Show in detail from this story how Tennyson accounts for Elaine's "fantasy."
   c. What touches reveal the character of Lancelot?
   d. Compare :
      (1.) Enid and Elaine.
      (2.) Geraint and Lancelot.
      (3.) The change in Arthur's court since the time of Geraint, as shown in this Idyll.
      (4.) The relation of either knight to the king.
   e. How many times in this story is the beauty of the scene enhanced by the natural beauties associated with it? Give the list of instances and discuss each briefly.
7. Why is the reader more interested in going with Lancelot when he leaves the castle than in staying with Elaine?
8. In the descriptive narrrative of this incident, what impression, what atmosphere, did Tennyson wish to create from many complex elements in the mind of the reader?
9. In the description of the ride of Lancelot and Lavaine, what points did Tennyson wish to impress on the reader?
10. What part of the journey remains most clearly defined in the readers' mind?
11. What was the poet's artistic purpose in the atmosphere and setting of this journey?
12. Where was the court when the joust for the diamonds was proclaimed?
13. Where, geographically, was Astolat?
14. Where was the tournament held?

NOTE.— Malory gives the geographical situation of these places in book xviii., chapter viii. Tennyson follows Malory in his geography, but the reader should note that the modern spelling of Malory's ' Gilford ' is Guilford.

15. Does the description of the tournament contribute to the development of the plot in the Idyll? In the Cycle? Give points in detail.
16. In what lies the artistic skill of the description of this joust for the diamonds?
17. Analyze the impression of life in Arthur's court at this time and show from whence each element of it is derived.

Gawain's quest; the trust betrayed:

18. *a.* Why did Gawain go to Astolat?
    b. Discuss the character of Gawain.
    (1.) In previous Idylls,
    (2.) In his relation to Arthur,
    (3.) In this story,
    (4.) In Tennyson's story, in what lay the root of failure in Gawain's character?
    c. When Gawain returned to court,
    (1.) How did the king receive his report?
    (2.) What was the effect of the news that he brought?

NOTE.— In the earliest versions of the Arthurian legends Gawain was the ideal of honor, courtesy, and virtue, trusted and beloved of the king. In later versions, especially in those modified by ecclesiastical influence, his character underwent a remarkable degeneration; he becomes treacherous, cruel, sensual. Malory compiled his romance from various sources without taking the pains necessary to reconcile inconsistencies; hence, it is the earlier Gawain who appears in one book, and the later in another, according to the source from which the story is translated, or adapted. Tennyson in *Idylls of the King*, disregards even more than Malory the just aspect of the characters in the stories he borrows, and more than once, for his own artistic end, he has given a sinister meaning to a beautiful mediaeval tale originally designed to express simply some natural impulse of human nature. Gawain is thus a victim of poetic necessity, and the explanation of the role assigned him must be sought in the purpose and unity of the series regarded as a carefully planned and consistently arranged whole. References for advanced students of this topic are given on p. 21.

The Quest of Elaine:

19.   *a.* The excuse for it; the real reason.
    b. When did Elaine first guess that Lancelot 'loved her not'?
    c. Could the knight have prevented the maid from setting her heart upon him?
    d. What was the nature and source of Lancelot's love for Elaine?
20. What purposes in the development of the plot does Elaine's quest serve?
21. What incident in the quest is most significant? What critical test shows this?
22. Is Elaine's request for love a blemish in a beautiful character? What was the author's purpose in that incident?

The Queen's Anger:

23.   *a.* Trace the relation of Lancelot and the queen as shown in each Idyll from the beginning.
    b. From what sources did danger threaten them at this time?
    c. What moved Guinevere to throw away the diamonds?
24. How did the king understand Elaine's letter?
25. What was the effect of the letter upon Lancelot? Upon the Queen?
26. How did the king understand the "homeless trouble" in the eyes of Lancelot? What remedy did he propose?
27. Three causes of grief wrought in Lancelot's mind as he sat by the river; which one seems to you the bitterest root of grief?
28. What is the theme of the Idyll as a separate episode?
29. Where do you find the climax of the dramatic action?
30. In what lies the real conclusion of the action?
31. What is the true relation of Elaine to Lancelot; that is, in his life, what does she represent?

32. In the story of Elaine's life, what would be the climax? What the conclusion?

In the Cycle:

33. What is the theme of this Idyll in the cycle?
34. Make an outline of the plot elements belonging to the cycle.
35. Compare the cycle plot, in "Lancelot and Elaine" with that of the episode:
    a. The beginning of each : show why one beginning is found at a point different from that of the other?
    b. Arrangement of antecedent material,—how does this differ in the two plots? Why?
    c. Theme : what is it in each?
    d. In what essential steps do the two plots differ? Explain the reason for each difference.
    e. Climax : in what is the climax of the part of the plot belonging in the cycle?
    f. Conclusion : show the relation of the conclusion in the episode to that of the plot elements belonging in the cycle. In each conclusion, show the critical reason that confirms your opinion.
36. What is the purpose of the character of Elaine in the cycle?
37. Why were Percivale and Galahad the knights to lift Elaine's body?
38. What is the importance of the barge in the story of Elaine's life?
39. What purposes in the cycle plot does the barge fulfill?
40. How does Tennyson account for the queen's loving Lancelot instead of Arthur?
41. What was the queen's own excuse for letting her love decline upon Lancelot?
42. What was Lancelot's own conception, in the beginning, of his love for the queen?
43. How was his resolution broken?

44. Had Arthur, at this point, any suspicion, either of the queen, or of Lancelot?

45. Analyze the inner strife of Lancelot's heart with which this Idyll concludes, showing the elements of it.

NOTE.— The conclusion of the drama enacted must be sought in an act, but in Tennyson's Idylls, subtly complex, the inner strife is truly a plot element, and its significance here must be in relation to the deeper meaning of the series. In Malory's story, this incident of Elaine follows the queste for the Grail; Tennyson shows fine artistic skill in placing it before that time. Lancelot's query "would I, if she willed it?" gains peculiar force from his prescience of the time of trial coming on, and by a word, the poet reveals, deep in the heart of the knight, a redeeming love of holiness.

46. Characteristics of Lancelot: This is note-book work, a character study of Lancelot, with references from the beginning of the Idylls, for the purpose of showing Tennyson's intention in the presentation of this character. Question for discussion;—is Lancelot the real hero of the Idylls, the greatest knight?

47. Characteristics of Arthur: Note-book work as above. Question for discussion; is Arthur an idealization, or has he passions and emotions in common with his fellows? In the author's plan, what is the relation of Arthur's character to the characters of the other knights?

48. Characteristics of Guinevere: Question, is she the great queen? What was her relation to Arthur's plan?

NOTE.— In this Idyll there is a closer relation than in any since "The Coming of Arthur" between the artistic subject, or theme, of the Idyll as a separate incident and the purpose of the story in the cycle. For this reason, the mingling plots are more intricate in their arrangement. In the Idyll, the true subject is *Lancelot and Elaine*; Sir Lancelot's relation to Elaine, which was her death, was to him the revelation of all that he had lost through the guilty love he bore the queen. The emphasis is placed upon the virginal love of the maid which, had he, the great knight, been also pure, might have brought him peace and "noble issue." In the greater story of the cycle, 'the face that came between' assumes significance; the love of Guinevere, to which, once given, he must be utterly loyal, was the active cause that prevented any love, that of Elaine, or of another, in his heart. It was love's lost opportunity and love's curse that weighed upon the man who knew that he was also a disloyal friend, as he sat in 'a cove by the river' and strove with himself.

LANCELOT AND ELAINE. PART II.

A few years since, "Lancelot and Elaine" was presented in *tableaux-vivant* by the Boston Alumnae of Smith College. The selection and description of suitable tableaux may be used as a study of the accuracy and detail of Tennyson's descriptions. The limitations of tableaux and also of pictorial art for the presentation of narrative should be considered; the sequence of incidents in the poem, on the one hand, and of the scenes selected on the other, should be compared for the purpose of discovering the conditions imposed by each form of art. In *Thoughts About Art*, by Philip Gilbert Hammerton, chapter v., " Word Painting and Color Painting," the student will find a most suggestive discussion of the limitations of pictorial and of literary art. There is also a discussion of Tennyson as an artist in word-description, in which he is compared with Ruskin, Shelley, and Wordsworth.

Tableaux may be given dramatic significance by the selection of scenes coinciding with moments of dramatic importance in the plot, or they may be arranged as idyllic pictures in which the scene suggests the narrative to those familiar with the poem. The requirement of art in tableaux is parallel with that of pictorial art; the scene must have a certain significance and be composed to express this meaning clearly; every smallest detail must be arranged with reference to this purpose, and there must be unity such that the parts compose to the eye a single effective picture, beautiful to look upon, and full of meaning.

49. If the tableaux of scenes in "Lancelot and Elaine" are to form a sequence, three subjects are possible:
  a. The story of Elaine's hopeless love.
  b. The Queen's Jealousy.
  c. Lancelot's story: 'The face that came between.'

As a study in narrative sequence:

50. a. Make from this Idyll a separate outline for each of these subjects, as a narrative.
  b. Show the completeness and unity of your arrangement of incidents by pointing out the beginning, the climax, the conclusion, for each subject.
  c. In selecting scenes to represent any one narrative sequence given above in the form of tableaux, what changes in arrangement, etc., would be neccessary?

NOTE.— These changes will be such as arise from the limitation of pictorial art as a means of narration.

IDYLLIC QUALITIES IN LANCELOT AND ELAINE.

The poem, Lancelot and Elaine, is full of pictures in words, and of bits of description which carry the imagination far afield,— the wild wave, "green glimmering toward the summit;" the "poplars with their noise of falling showers;" "the vine clad oriel;" "the pictured wall." In study of these passages, there is an opportunity to fix in the mind the difference between the idyllic picture which is essential to the progress of the narrative and those bits of description that serve merely as a setting, background, or accompaniment of the tale. The words idyll, or idyllic, as signifying a type of poem, or a poetic quality, should be avoided. The meaning connoted by these terms is most composite and difficult of definition. The teacher herself, if without special advanced training, may be pardoned for hesitation or uncertainty in these distinctions. Everyone who reads, however, may select from the narrative those exquisite descriptions which, like the picture of the artist, have an organization and arrangement of detail significant in meaning. The material is that of the artist; the meaning is an essential element in the narrative. Such a picture is the one in which the maid of Astolat stands by the gate, her bright hair blown about her face; such another is the description of Elaine appearing before Lancelot in the early morning while he thought, "he had not dreamed she was so beautiful." This passage might be reckoned a bit of pure description,— the morning light, the face of the maid, innocent and fair as an opening blossom, rapt with the love that was her doom,— were it not that the moment is of significance in three lives. Elaine gazes on the face of her knight as if it were a god's and thereafter would choose death rather than let her love decline on any other than God's best and greatest. Lancelot, seeing her so sweet and true, realizes for a moment that such a love as hers might have brought him happiness and "noble issue, sons born to the glory of his name and fame." Here, also, the rumor that stirred such bitter pain in the heart of the queen took its rise, in the acceptance by Lancelot of the sleeve embroidered with pearls.

The critical test should be found in the intimacy of the relation. The fact that a poem contains beautiful descriptions does not make it an Idyll. The idyllic setting must be essential to the proper presentation of the subject, and the narrative must be attuned in spirit and in the manner of telling to the background, or setting.

Written descriptions of scenes or studies will aid greatly in defining the quality and use of the word-pictures; these descriptions should take the form of imaginative memoranda for the artist who is to illustrate the text, and details merely suggested or implied in the poem, should be fully specified in the directions. Incidentally, this sort of composition will define an essential difference between description in words and description with pencil or brush. When the significance of the picture is an important element in the story this should be suggested and all directions should aim at an arrangement of detail in the portrayal that will emphasize the meaning. For other pictures, the writer of directions should simply define the dominant note or purpose in the description; in descriptions that are little pictures by the way, the inquiry must be for the impression the poet wished to convey; for, in Tennyson's verse, each bit holds some intimate relation to the whole poem.

The order of selection for this study is suggested below but the successful result will depend upon the time given to the passages chosen by the pupils, and the imaginative realization of the detail in each. Written descriptions of scenes or studies will aid greatly in defining the quality and use of the word-pictures in the poem. These may take the form of memoranda for an artist who is to illustrate the text. Freedom must be granted in the imagination of details merely suggested, or implied, in the poem.*

The order of selection for this study is:

51. *a.* All pictures which form a part of the narrative; such as the picture of the queen throwing away the pearls.

    b. All pictures which, if painted, would involve some composition or arrangement of parts; such as King Arthur at the tournament.

    c. All descriptions which may be called studies; for instance, of the faintly shadowed track winding up where the towers of Astolat showed against the western sky.

52. Do you consider, after this study, the poem, "Lancelot and Elaine," an Idyll, or an idyllic poem?

NOTE.— See also the topics given on pages 54-5, "Merlin and Vivien," for study of idyllic qualities, and of the Idyll as a literary form. Use the same topics here, in addition to those given above as tests, and in the result arrange a critical comparison of the two poems with illustrations and argument.

53. What emotions did Tennyson attempt to portray in Lancelot and Elaine?

NOTE.— Trace and note the different phases of emotion described or suggested, as you would trace a plot development. Compare with "Merlin and Vivien" in this respect.

* In part, quoted from an essay by the editor on the teaching of Lancelot and Elaine.

54. Compare "Lancelot and Elaine" with "Merlin and Vivien," in regard to:
   a. Literary qualities.
   b. Idyllic setting.
   c. Dramatic or narrative interest and power.
   d. The presentation of character.
   e. The description and suggestion of emotion.
   f. The appeal to the imagination:—how do you test the poem in regard to this quality?

NOTE.— These two poems are especially fine for critical comparison in that the one presents a beautiful and pathetic story that enlists the sympathy of all, while the other reveals the secret working of evil influences, and repels. The reader must, therefore, distinguish between liking and admiration and those qualities that arise from a fine literary sense, creative genius, or perfect mastery of the means of expression.

The individual should select but one of the topics suggested and on this prepare her study, which may be presented either as a brief discussion from a carefully prepared outline, or as a written paper.

55. Mark in this poem any passages remarkable for *Vision*.
56. Select the finest extended descriptive passages, and name them in order of excellence in beauty and literary quality, with reasons for your judgment.
57. Do you notice any qualities, or characteristics, belonging especially to Tennyson's descriptions?

THE HOLY GRAIL.

NOTE.— For the growth of the Grail Saga, see Ten Brink's Early English Literature, pp. 171-4; The Flourishing of Romance, chapter iii.; English Writers, book iii., pp. 120-148. A good translation of *Le conte du Grail* is published in the Temple Classics. The translator says that "In very truth, the story of the Holy Grail here told is not only the most coherent and poetic of all the many versions of the Legend, but is also the first and most authentic."

For Tennyson's hesitation in regard to this Idyll, see Memoir, ii., p. 126. For his interpretation of his own work, see Memoir, ii., 63, 65, 126-7, 53.

The Grail in Malory's *Le Morte Darthur*:
The birth of Galahad, book xi., chapters i., ii., vi., viii.
Galahad knighted, book xiii., chapters i., ii., iii., iv., v.
Galahad takes the siege, book xiii., chapters iii., iv.
Galahad's adventures, book xiii., chapters ix., x., xii., xiii., xvii.
    book xviii., chapters i.-xiv., xviii.-xxiii.
Lancelot's madness, book xi., chapter viii.
    book xii., chapters i., iv., v.-x.
  adventures, book xiii., chapters viii.-xx.
    book xv., chapters i.-vi.
Percivale's life, book i., chapter xxii.
    book x., chapter xxiii.
    book xi., chapters xi.-xiv.; xi., chapters vii.-viii.
    book xiii., chapter iii., and book xiv.
Percivale's adventures, book xi., chapters x., xii., xiii., xiv.
    book xii., chapter viii.
    book xiv., chapters i.-vi., x.
    book xvii., chapter ix.-xi.
Percivale's sister, book xvii., chapters ix.-xi.
The departure, book xiii., chapters vi.-viii.
Gawain's adventures, book xvi., chapters i.-v.
Sir Bors' adventures, book xvi., chapters vi.-xvii.
See also *Arthur and the Round Table*, by W. W. Newell.

PRELIMINARY TOPICS.

The Tradition of the Grail:
1. Its historical origin.
2. How the Grail came to England and the traditions of its place of concealment, and its miraculous powers.

The story of the Grail in literature;
3. A historical sketch for general information and for reference.

The story of the Grail in art:
4. This topic is suggested here merely for illustration; the pictures of Abbey's mural decoration in the Boston public library, and the stage pictures of Wagner's *Parzival*, are especially interesting.

TENNYSON'S QUEST OF THE HOLY GRAIL.
5. Read the entire Idyll for general outline, impression, and beauty, before beginning special study.
6. What is the point of view from which the plot is presented?
7. For what reason was this point of view chosen by the author?
8. What supernatural powers were attributed to the Grail?

NOTE.—The supernatural powers of the Grail, in the belief of the middle ages, is an interesting topic for the special student but will call for investigation and study in the library far beyond the requirements for the critical study of Tennyson's Idyll.

9. What traditions about the Grail did Tennyson make essential to his dramatic presentation?
10. Where is the real beginning of the plot?
11. When the Grail returned to earth, who had seen it first? The fulfillment of what conditions brought the vision? Who was chosen next? Why?

NOTE.—For the condition of receiving the vision in Malory's tale, see book xiii., chapter viii.

12. When the Grail re-appeared among men, what means was chosen for transmitting zeal for this quest from person to person? Why?
13. Which is significant in the plot, Arthur's absence when the Grail appeared, or the cause of it?
14. In Malory's story, where was the king at this time? *Morte Darthur*, book xiii., chapter vii.
15. How does Tennyson's description of the appearance of the Grail differ from Malory's? *Morte Darthur*, book xiii., chapter vii.
16. What was Arthur's thought about the Grail? How do you explain the difference between his attitude toward the quest and that of his knights? What is the meaning in lines 293–
17. Why had the Siege Perilous never been filled? Had any attempted to sit in it?
18. What is the significance of the "Siege Perilous" in the plot? What is the meaning of it allegorically?
19. Has there been any special preparation for the subject of this Idyll in previous Idylls?

NOTE.—Seek the answer to this question in study of every reference, in previous Idylls, to the religion of King Pellam. The ascetic devotees of mysticism, in the dark ages, looked for some miraculous source of healing for the perils and evils of the time. It was the secret thought of the king that, when the hearts of men became clean 'the holy thing' would return and dwell, once more, on earth; in the condition, lo! in the clean hearts, lay the secret of the world's healing.

20. How do you define and explain the character of Galahad and the feeling of the knights toward him?
21. What is the significance of placing the description of Merlin's hall in close connection with the dispersal of Arthur's knights on this quest?
22. What is the connection between the intimacy of Lancelot and the queen, and Lancelot's desire to join the quest for the Grail?

23. Why is the queen's word, "this madness," introduced at the point of the narrative where it is found?
24. Tennyson has changed the order of events from the time of the appearance of Galahad to the departure of the knights, and in so doing he omits the going to the minster to hear service, which Mr. Abbey has chosen as the subject of one of the largest of his pictures.
   a. What, in outline, is the order of incidents as given in *Morte Darthur?*
   b. What was Tennyson's reason for changing this order, and for omitting the service in the Minster?

NOTE.—This reason must lie in the significance of this quest of the Grail in the large drama of human effort and experience, unfolded, for the attentive mind, idyll by idyll. Tennyson's indebtedness to Malory in the description of the knights riding through the streets amidst weeping, is marked.

Percivale's Quest:

25. Tennyson once said that the key to the mystical treatment of his subject in this Idyll is to be found in a careful reading of Sir Percivale's vision, and subsequent fall, and nineteenth century temptations.
   a. What special hindrance or difficulty in the way of Percivale's success in the beginning of his quest?
   b. What temptations beset him? How was each overcome, or escaped? What is the allegorical meaning of each?
   c. How did Percivale become worthy of the vision?
26. What means did Tennyson choose for the transmission of the passion for the Grail to Galahad? Why?
27. Show in detail if you can, whether Galahad's quest represents:
   a. The pursuit of an ideal by an individual, or
   b. Mysticism in religion, in the church, in the middle ages.

28. Compare Percivale's temptations:
   a. Which appealed most strongly to a man of his nature and disposition? Why?
   b. Which one did Tennyson represent as falling upon the greatest number of persons at the present time?
   c. How did Percivale finally escape his temptations and win a sight of the Grail?
29. What is the relation of the quest of Galahad to the quest of the other knights? To Arthur's ideal?
30. What is the signifiance of the bridge at the close of Galahad's quest?
31. Why must the quest of Galahad, alone, end in the invisible city?
32. Is the disappearance of the Grail in the city significant in the dramatic presentation, in the artistic quality, or in the allegorical meaning of this Idyll?

Note on the quest of Galahad.—The words of Arthur, lines 885— must be read in connection with this account of the disappearance of the Grail and of Galahad. Tennyson touches lightly, but reverently upon the historical significance of the Grail,—in times past, it had been seen by such as the nun and this virgin knight; with the passing of mysticism, the Grail had withdrawn into the holy city, and thenceforward, represented, the unseen ideals of the higher life. The ideal can never be attained; even as the seeker catches some glimpses of its beauty, it withdraws until at length the follower of the gleam is lured on into the invisible city.

33. Sir Bors' Quest:
   a. Why did Sir Bors seem least likely to achieve the vision?
   b. What motive sent him forth?
   c. To what, in himself, was the distant vision due?

NOTE.—Sir Bors bound by earthly ties of human love, was no mystic; yet led by unselfish devotion to Lancelot, his brother, he, at length, saw a distant vision of the Grail and found the reward of his quest because his love, though physical and human, was full of service. Perhaps no other knight fulfilled a part more truly in accord with Arthur's ideal.

34. Sir Gawain's Quest:
   a. What motives sent him?
   b. Why did he fail in the quest?
   c. What is the part of Gawain's character in the cycle of the Idylls?
   See also the note on the character of Gawain, page 58.
35. Did Lancelot hope to achieve the quest when he set out? Why did he go?
36. What was Malory's story of the adventures of Lancelot?
37. In the story of Lancelot's adventures as given by Tennyson, explain the meaning of each part as far as you are able, and show how through them he came near to the Grail.
38. The judgments of King Arthur:
   a. Name each one and show what in the knight's character brought it forth.
   b. Discuss each with reference to the theme of the Idyll.
   Tennyson's interpretation of these judgments is in Memoir, ii., 63.
39. What is the theme of the "Holy Grail" as a separate Idyll?
40. Make an outline of the plot of the Idyll, and consider the significance of each part in relation to the theme.
41. Where is the beginning of the plot of the story told by Percivale.
42. In what is the climax of this plot?
43. What is the conclusion of it?

The Holy Grail in the Cycle:

44. Why did Tennyson include "The Holy Grail" in the plan of the Idylls?
45. What were the difficulties in the way of its presentation?
46. How is this purpose connected with the dramatic presentation of the plot of which Queen Guinevere is the center?

47. What plot elements belonging to the cycle are found in "The Holy Grail"?
48. What descriptive passages and character studies in "The Holy Grail" are important parts of the Cycle?
49. What is the significance of the sculpture that adorned Camelot?
50. What is the significance of the final withdrawal of the Grail from the earth at the close of this quest?
51. Who is the hero of the quest in Tennyson's tale?
Who is the hero in *Le Morte Darthur?*
52. *a.* What was Arthur's secret hope in reference to the Grail?
  b. How might it have been fulfilled?
  c. What causes, working secretly, rendered this hope futile?

In the last poetic paragraph of "The Holy Grail" in which the king speaks of his work and his visions Tennyson intended to sum up all the spiritual meaning of the Idylls "in the highest note, by the highest of human men." Memoir ii., 90.

53. *a.* In these words Arthur suggests the real reason why he could not join in the quest,—what was it?
  b. Arthur also explains the secret purpose and vision of his own life; explain this in your own phrases, or find other passages in the Idylls that interpret this one.
54. What is the meaning of the character of Galahad in the cycle? What was his part in relation to the Knights of the Round Table? In relation to Arthur.
55. What is the importance of "The Holy Grail" in the cycle of the Idylls? Show the relation of this Idyll to the preceding ones. How is the special theme of "The Holy Grail" subordinated to the dramatic action running through the cycle?
56. Compare "The Holy Grail" and Wagner's *Parzival* in:
  a. Theme. *c.* Ethical purpose.
  b. Plot, or dramatic development. *d.* Realism and idealism.

57. Poetic qualities:

    a. What is the prevailing impression or "tone," of "The Holy Grail"? Show how this impression is imparted,— by what artistic or literary qualities.

    b. What passages seem to you most noble? Why?

    c. What passages seem to you most beautiful? Why?

NOTE.— The topics for critical study of Tennyson's use of the old tales may be found in the references given above, and the topics suggested for this study in earlier Idylls will serve as a guide. The study by analysis and comparison of noble, or beautiful, or pregnant passages of this idyll, may be valuable in increasing appreciation of literary beauty and in fixing in the mind parts best worth remembering. In the selection and comparison of passages of special literary excellence, each must use his own tests and appeal in the final resort to his own standards of taste. The following queries, or tests are no more than suggestions, and in using them the student must be aware that in the criticism of art, it is the spirit and the understanding that give life.

58. *a.* Has the passage a noble meaning, or conception, as its central purpose?

    b. Does it appeal to the imagination, and stimulate the reader?

    c. Is it marked by "Vision" of a high order?

    d. Is it complex, composed of meaning folded within meaning, of many details, or swift transitions?

    e. Has it organization of parts, is it marked by point of view, beginning, progress toward some point corresponding in a degree to climax; is there selection and subordination of details in the arrangement?

PELLEAS AND ETTARRE.

The Old Tale:

Le Morte Darthur: book iv., chapters xx., xxi.-xxiii.
For the character of Sir Gawain and the changes through which it passed in mediaeval literature, see *The Legend of Sir Gawain, Studies upon its Original Scope and Significance*, by Jessie L. Weston. Also, *The Flourishing of Romance*, by George Saintsbury, p. 114.

English Writers, by Henry Morley, vol. iii., p. 279; vol. vi., pp. 59, 240; and Syr Gawayne and the Greene Knight.

For Gawain in *Le Morte Darthur*, book vii., chapter xxxv.; book x., chapter lviii.; book xiii., chapter xvi.; book xx., chapter i.

"In Pelleas and Ettarre," the mingling plots bring forward with greater emphasis than heretofore the characters and motives of the cycle which is now moving rapidly toward a moment of catastrophe. In the Idyll, the theme is repeated in the refrain of the song, "He dies who loves it — if the worm be there." Sir Pelleas, young, noble, drawn to Arthur's court, as was Gareth in an earlier time, in search of an ideal, saw the form of beauty and worshiped it, and so was lost and needs must die, since his love and the queen and all the Table Round were false. The end seems, indeed, at hand when we see Pelleas fleeing in the gloom of night and hear him yelling "Why, then, let men couple at once with wolves." In the cycle, the purpose of this Idyll may be phrased in the words of Lancelot, 'The sword between the lips.' To the guilty queen and her lover, the incident was a warning of the dolorous day to be. For the reader, it marks the wide difference between the ideals of life in Camelot in early days and the evil times that had befallen.

Topics for Study:

1. Make, for use in topics given below, a plot outline of Pelleas and Ettarre as an Idyll.

2. The Story of Pelleas and Ettarre in *Le Morte Darthur*:
   a. Make an outline of this story as given by Malory, showing the beginning, antecedent series of adventures, climax, and conclusion.
   b. In *Morte Darthur*, where, in the chronology of Arthur's life, is the advent of Sir Pelleas to the fellowship of the Round Table placed?
   c. What drew him to Arthur? For what reasons did he claim admission to the order?
3. Which of the adventures used as the material of Tennyson's Idylls came earlier in Malory's tale than the advent of Sir Pelleas?
4. Compare Sir Pelleas, at the time he came to Court, with the young knight, Gareth when he came, in, —
   a. Original in *Le Morte Darthur*.
   b. Reasons for coming.
   c. Personal character, ideals, and ambition.
   d. Adventures.
   e. Personal relation to Arthur, the king.
   f. Feeling toward Guinevere.
   g. Influence of the knights of the Round Table, and of the Queen upon the young Knight.
5. For what does the character of Pelleas stand in Tennyson's mind?
6. Trace the character of Sir Gawain through the Idylls, thus far, making a character study.
7. What reputation had the knight, Sir Gawain, among the knights of the Round table in *Le Morte Darthur?* In *Idylls of the King?*
8. Has the character of Ettarre any special purpose with reference to Arthur's court and fellowship?
9. How many times in the series of Idylls has Modred appeared? Each time, for what? Has his appearance here any special meaning?

10. What is the real subject, or theme of Pelleas and Ettarre, as n Idyll?
11. In what is the beginning of the plot?
12. What is the significance of the madness that came on Pelleas?
13. What is the meaning of the song in relation to the plot of the Idyll.
14. Where is the climax of this Idyll?
15. This Idyll was published in 1869; before the edition of 1894, Tennyson had added lines 386-406. Show why they were added by discussing the content of the lines, and also the respects in which they modify or interpret other parts of this Idyll?
16. What is the conclusion of this Idyll?
17. Why could not Tennyson use the denouement in Malory's story?

In the Cycle:

18. Mark in the plot outline of the Idyll all plot elements found in this Idyll which belong to the series.
19. What is the purpose of "Pelleas and Ettarre" in the series?
20. What incidents, characters, etc., have a different significance and value in the series from that in the Idyll?
21. In the series, what is the special significance,
    a. Of the Song?
    b. Of the tournament?
    c. Of the form of madness that came on Pelleas?
    d. Of the incident between Pelleas and Lancelot?
22. In the series, which are the chief characters in this incident?
23. What is the climax of the incident regarded as an act of the drama?
24. What is the conclusion?
25. Compare Pelleas with Balin in,
    a. The cause of his madness.
    b. The effect of his discovery on the mind.

26. What is the significance of the outcome as marking the difference between the time of Balin and the time of Pelleas? This Idyll follows "The Holy Grail" and in it the poet intended to utter a warning of the doom that was coming ever nearer, and to summarize, as it were, all the influences working together for the disintegration and decay of the Order of the Round Table, and, thus, for the frustration of Arthur's hope and purpose.

27. *a.* Show analytically all the influences gradually undermining the ideals of life and conduct at Camelot; trace each back to the beginning of it, and show what the results have thus far been.
   b. At this time, how did the knights regard King Arthur, and his ideal of knighthood?
   c. How did they understand the vows formerly taken?
   d. How did the knights excuse their own failures?
   f. What connection was there between this changed attitude of the knights and the dispersal to seek the Grail?

Literary Qualities:

28. Select the scenes in "Pelleas and Ettarre" which are specially idyllic in setting and description. For each show:
   a. The dramatic elements of the scene.
   b. The idyllic elements of the scene, and the reasons for the selection of these; that is, the character and effect of the idyllic setting in relation to the chief purpose of the scene in the narrative.

29. Select the descriptions in "Pelleas and Ettarre," most beautiful in themselves, apart from their relation to the narrative? In what, chiefly, lies the beauty of the passages you select?

30. Consider critically all figures of speech asking:
   a. Which is most perfect? Why?
   b. Which is most beautiful? Why?
   c. Which appeals most strongly to the imagination? How do you show this?

d. Which most perfectly suits the purpose of its introduction in illustrating and adorning some element of the narrative?

NOTE.— Subordination to the idea for the sake of which the figure is introduced is one element of perfect suitability. The term "extended figures of speech" is intended to include all figures, but not figurative language, words, or phrases, forming an integral part of sentences having another purpose.

Vowel harmonies:

31. Select four or five passages which illustrate the beauty that may be given to verse by selection and variation of vowel sounds. Show why the arrangement pleases. Has the effect thus given the lines any special relation to the meaning expressed? Has alliteration any part in the effect?

For comparison of harmony of sound in poetry with the same quality in prose, see the discussion of this topic in an essay "On some Technical Elements of style in Literature," by R. L. Stevenson.

THE LAST TOURNAMENT.

The Old Story:

The eighth book of *Le Morte Darthur* is devoted to the adventures of Tristram. The references given here are to those parts of the tale which have to do with La Beale Isoud. The tenth book in Malory's narrative is called the second book of Sir Tristram.

Book viii., chapters iii., ix., x., xi., xii., xix., xxiv., xxix., xxx., xxxi., xxxii., xxxiv.—xxxvii.

Book x., chapters l., lii., lxv., lxx.—lxvii., lxxxi., lxxxviii.

The magic cup, see book viii., chapter xxiv.

The magic horn, see book vii., chapter xxxiv.

The Tristram Saga, see The Flourishing of Romance by George Saintsbury, p. 116.

Studies in Arthurian Legend, by Rhys, pp. 12, 37, etc.

The use of the Tristram story by Arnold in *Tristram and Iseult*, by Swinburne in *Tristram of Lyonesse*, and by Wagner in *Tristan* is not included in this study. It belongs, properly, in a study of the Arthurian Legends in modern literature.

NOTE.—The incidents, characters, and arrangement of the narrative in "The Last Tournament" are entirely determined by the purpose of the author in the development of the series. As a separate Idyll, it has no unity or completeness of plot structure. In the Idyll, Tristram is the central figure ; but in the cycle, his character is not essential to the main action ; at most, it fulfills a purpose of illustration and presents typically, a theory of life which Tennyson adapts to his own use. The beautiful mediæval story of the love of Tristram and Iseult, he uses as a parallel, in baser and more sensual form, of the loves of Lancelot and the great queen, thus showing the depth of corruption following in the wake of sin, such as theirs. In truth, in the last Idylls of the series the dramatic action running through all becomes more important and fixes the attention, almost to the exclusion of interest in the separate Idyll. It is, therefore, natural that the author, unfailing in artistic skill, merges one story in the other to such a degree that the narrative of the Idyll becomes merely the medium used to forward the great action of the series. In " The Last Tournament," the semblance of a separate story remains ; The subject of the tale is Tristram, the " broken music' of his life being an illustration and a proof of the moral contamination which had spread even to distant parts of Arthur's realm through the queen and Lancelot. In the incident, Tristram is the main character, but in this great act of the drama of the cycle, Arthur is the central figure who in the moment of catastrophe, at the close, is left alone on the stage. In " Guinevere " and in " The passing of Arthur," the main dramatic action, so long intermingled with the incidents of separate narratives, becomes the subject of the Idyll. The poignant greatness of the tragedy in Guinevere is heightened by the cumulative force of many and complex elements ; the reader yields his mind to it as one who, following devious waterways for a long time, at length, feels himself borne out toward the infinite deep upon some great tidal current. In considering the relation of plot elements in Idyll and cycle, the order of study followed in the earlier part of the series is reversed.

1. Make an outline of the plot elements of the cycle found in the story of "The Last Tournament."
2. Make an outline of the separate story or episode of "The Last Tournament".
3. What is the theme of the Idyll, "The Last Tournament"?
4. What plot elements in this Idyll are important in the cycle?
5. Why did Tennyson place the beginning of "The Last Tournament" on the morning after it took place?
6. In what is the beginning of the action?
7. Show the purpose in the Idyll of each part of the antecedent material produced.
8. At what point is the action of this Idyll resumed?
9. Trace the part of Sir Dragonet through the Idyll and show the purpose for which Tennyson uses this character. The explanation must include his words and their meaning with reference to the development of the main plot of the series.
10. What is the reason for the introduction of a counter-round table?
11. Why is the account of Arthur's quest given as an interlude in Tristram's journey?
12. Is Tristram's song," Free-love—free field," significant chiefly in the story of Tristram and Isolt, or in the series of the Idylls? Show reasons for your opinion in the artistic structure of the narrative.
13. What is the interpretation to be given to Tristram's song before Isolt, "Ay, ay, oh, ay"?
14. What is the artistic purpose of this song in the Idylls?
15. What is the difference between Isolt's excuse for yielding to love and Guinevere's?
16. What was Tristram's theory of life? Of love?
17. Are the morality and theories of "The Last Tournament" borrowed from the old tales or invented by Tennyson?

18. What was Tristram's opinion of Arthur? Of Arthur's vows? What was his explanation of the change in Arthur's court?
19. What other opinions of Arthur have been given?
20. Character study of Lancelot:
    a. His ideals.
    b. His early purpose with regard to Guinevere; to Arthur.
    c. The cause of change.
    d. Lancelot's position and influence in the court.
21. Trace Lancelot's inner life through the Idylls in such a way as to show the quality of the man's spirit, his strength and weakness, the secret of each, his greatest mistake, the denial of himself that cost him most, his inmost desire.
22. What is the difference between Arthur's meaning in the words, "It it well?" and Lancelot's understanding of them?
23. Has there been, hitherto, in the Idylls, any sign that Arthur entertained a suspicion of Lancelot, or of Guinevere?
24. How do you explain the turning of the queen's thought to Arthur in this time of doubt and pain?
25. Why is the account of Arthur's quest given as an interlude in Tristram's journey?
26. There is in this Idyll more than one parallel suggested between the love of Isolt and Tristram and the love of the Queen and Lancelot; note these suggestions and inquire what Tennyson's purpose was in the complexion given this story.
27. How is the Queen's flight told? Why? What is the significance of this moment in the cycle?
28. What is the significance of "The Last Tournament," in the series of the Idylls? What incident in the Idyll is most important in the cycle plot? Why?
29. Select one of the following poetic qualities and make a study of it throughout the Idyll, as before.
    a. Figurative language.
    b. Beauty of Description.
    c. Suggestiveness and Vision.
    d. Rythmic beauty in the succession of vowel sounds?

GUINEVERE.

The Old Tale:

The conclusion of the love of Lancelot and Guinevere; in *Le Morte Darthur*, book xix., xx.
Modred's treason and Arthur's death, in book xxi.
See also Memoir, I., pp. 4, 19, 453.

TOPICS FOR STUDY.

Here, for the first time, the queen becomes the central figure of the story.

1. What is the beginning of this plot?
2. What antecedent material is introduced at different points? For what reasons? Why was it held back until the plot was so near a conclusion?
3. Does this revelation change the meaning of past incidents in the reader's mind?
4. In what respects does the story of the little maid differ from the narrative already given to the reader?
5. For what purpose is the song of the little maid used?
6. In Guinevere's own thought, what was the chief element of tragedy?
7. For what reason is the musing of Guinevere placed just before the coming of the king?
8. In Arthur's judgment of the queen, in what, chiefly, did he find her sin?
9. In what points is the judgment of the king significant in relation to Guinevere's inner life.
10. What grounds of hope, however distant, did he point out?
11. Why had Arthur failed to win the love of Guinevere, in the beginning?
12. Is the reason for the turning of Guinevere's love to Arthur, at the last, found in the character of the queen, in the plot, or in the theme, or artistic purpose, of the Idylls? Show the requirements in regard to each, and which had effect in the determination of the result.

13. What preparation in previous Idylls, if any, for Guinevere's turning to Arthur do you find? Is the preparation sufficient in the dramatic sense?
14. What is the artistic necessity for this change in relation to Tennyson's inner and spiritual meaning in the Idylls?
15. What was Guinevere's idea of repentance?
16. What was the difference between Guinevere's repentance and that of Lancelot?

NOTE.— A most interesting comparison between Lady Macbeth and Guinevere may be made at this point. Shakespeare and Tennyson have each shown the effect of a consciousness of guilt on the feminine and on the masculine mind.

17. What is the most dramatic moment in "Guinevere?" The most significant moment in the plot?
18. What scene in "Guinevere" is most effective for stage presentation?
19. What moment fixes in the reader's mind the sense of finality in the catastrophe?
20. Trace Modred through the cycle. What relation has this character to the progress of the plot?
21. Effectiveness in plot, in situations, depends, in great degree, upon preparation.. What preparation for cycle elements in the development of the plot in Guinevere has been made in previous Idylls?

Find these in:
- a. Characters common to all the Idyll's, on which the plot depends; discuss the relation of these to the plot, in the order of importance.
- b. *Momenti* tending to a climax and a conclusion. Show in which, chiefly, the main plot centers, and the relation of each subordinate *motif* to this central one.
- c. The artistic purpose of each Idyll in the series in relation to the one preceding and the one following.
- d. The epic presentation of King Arthur.
- e. The allegorical interpretation.

22. Critical question: Is there sufficient *preparation* for the turning of the queen's heart to Arthur, at the last?
23. What is Tennyson's final word about Arthur and the queen's love?
24. In *Le Morte Darthur*, book iii., chapter i., Malory includes a warning of evil to come, in his account of how Arthur wedded a wife. Why did Tennyson omit this warning in " The Coming of Arthur?" Show from the later development of the plot whether a forecast of possible danger, or the omission of any such hint, is the truer art.

The Significance of " Guinevere " in the Cycle.

25. Prepare for each previous Idyll, in order, a brief statement of its subject and artistic purpose in the series;
26. Of its chief significance in advancing the main plot of the series;
27. Of its relation and connection with previous Idylls.
28. In the great dramatic action running through the series,
   a. In what do you find the artistic purpose, or theme, of the cycle?
   b. Where do you place the climax of the action? Why?
   c. Where do you place the conclusion of the action? Why?

NOTE.— There are, appparently, two disintegrating forces at work among Arthur's followers. In form, one is subordinated to the other, but only slightly, so that in effect there is a divided climax, and a lessening of unity, but the gain in the expression of both spiritual and dramatic meaning in one narrative compensates for an apparent weakness in the formal arrangement of the plot. In the drama written for Sir Henry Irving, the effect of the whole is marred by the borrowing of scene and form without the deeper meaning which, in Tennyson's Idylls, gives such poignant significance to the moments of climax and conclusion.

29. Why did Tennyson place the death of Arthur after the conclusion of the Idylls?

For the fact that Tennyson recognized "Guinevere" as the the close of the Idylls, see Memoir, vol. ii., p. 126.

30. How did Malory conclude the dramatic action of *Le Morte Darthur*?
31. How did he conclude the love of Lancelot and Guinevere? Why?
32. Why did Malory include the death of Arthur in the dramatic action of his tale?
33. Who is the hero of *Idylls of the King*? What is the proof?
34. Who is the hero of Malory's story? What is the proof?

Literary Qualities:

35. Study the artistic setting employed to heighten the effectiveness of the scenes in Guinevere, showing:
    a. Selection in description.
    b. Relation of Idyllic and artistic setting to the character of the scene.
    c. Effect produced: Define, or characterize the effect; is it an aid or a detriment in relation to the dramatic quality of the action?

NOTE.—In Guinevere, as in no other Idyll, description, setting, even idyllic qualities, are used for dramatic effect; each must therefore be studied with reference to the character of the scene thus heightened or adorned. The selection and adjustment of idyllic material differs widely from that in poems where the natural features of the scene are used for pictorial effect, or mingle with the narrative intimately, forming thus the true Idyll. But Guinevere is, above all, a great tragic poem; the "atmosphere" of the descriptive passages is caught from the emotional content of the scenes, but setting and background soon slip out of mind, leaving in the memory only the deep pathos and significance of the dramatic story, and the figures of those who have suffered, the sorrow, pity, and the irretrievable loss.

THE PASSING OF ARTHUR.

The Old Story: Le Morte Darthur, Book xxi., chapters i., ii., iii., iv., v.

NOTE.—A brief narrative of the misfortunes that befell the king after the dispersal of his knights should be given by the instructor as an introduction to study of "The Passing of Arthur." The material from which it should be drawn will be found in the Idylls, in *Morte Darthur*, and in narrative versions, such as Newell's *King Arthur*,—an especially useful book. Attention should be centered upon Arthur, the king, his life, his death, his ideals.

The narrative of the rescue of Queen Guinevere from death by fire, of the wars between King Arthur and Lancelot on her account, is in book xx. of Malory's tale. The deaths of the queen in a nunnery, and of Lancelot, a holy man, at Canterbury, are reached by different incidents in the two versions. Tennyson selected, here and there, certain incidents of Malory's story suited to his own purpose, but his arrangement of parts embodies a tragic action and a meaning in no wise suggested in the old romance. Much of "The Passing of Arthur" is mystical in meaning and in no other Idyll is there such tangible evidence of the mingling of earlier and later conceptions in Tennyson's mind. "Morte D' Arthur,"— lines 170-440 of "The Passing of Arthur",—was published in "The Epic," in 1842, and had been composed about five years earlier. It narrates the passing of a great epic hero, gone to heal him of his wounds, destined, perchance, in some distant day, to return and fulfill, in happier times, his great purpose;—for "many men say that there is written upon his tomb this verse ' Hic jacet Arthurus Rex, quondam Rex que futurus.'" This Idyll in its present form was first published in 1869, but many changes and additions were made before the Library edition of Tennyson's poems in 1872 in which the Idylls, arranged in sequence, appeared. In the lines added or changed in this period, is found indisputable evidence of the poet's own interpretation of the inner meaning of the Idylls, mingling in

each and growing, toward the end, to clearer and fuller expression.
In the careful comparison of editions made by•Richard Jones, it
appears that lines 6 . . . 28, and 441 . . . 447, were added after the
publication of " The Passing of Arthur "; in 1869, probably about
1872, in connection with the arrangement in sequence of all the
Idylls then written.

It is natural, then, to divide the study of this Idyll into two
parts, one of the epic story which shows, even in the objective and
Homeric form of narration chosen for it, evidence of an inner
meaning, a spiritual purpose; the other, of the Idyll fulfilling the
purpose of the poet as the final and definite expression of the
meanings half revealed, half hidden, in the earlier Idylls.

TOPICS FOR STUDY.

"THE PASSING OF ARTHUR" AS AN EPIC STORY.

The Revolt in Arthur's Kingdom:

1. Who was Modred?
2. Trace Modred's career through all the Idylls and show the part he played in Arthur's Court.
3. What was his excuse for leading a rebellion against Arthur?

NOTE.— Malory names the parts of England — countries in the south — that joined Modred. Book xxi., chapter iii.

4. Where did he take his stand for the last fight?
5. Arthur's Sword, Excalibur:
    a. How came Arthur by the sword Excalibur in Tennyson's story? In Malory's story? See *Morte Darthur*, book i., chapter xxiii.
    b. For what was Arthur to use the sword?
6. Arthur's Presentiment:
    a. Read the moanings of the king overheard by Sir Bedivere. What causes of grief oppressed him at this time?
    b. Why did Arthur feel no hope or courage in going to battle at this time?

NOTE.—The Celts believed that the appearance of one near of kin, or very dear, betokened the approach of death. The voice of Gawain, "light upon the wind," seems an echo caught from Ossian's poems, in which many illustrations of the same belief may be found.

7. Who were the survivors of this fight?
8. Tell in your own words the story of the casting away of Excaliber. Why was Bedivere so loth to lose Arthur's sword?
9. What was the meaning of the sign that came to Arthur?
10. a. Read the account of Arthur's departure as an allegory with a spiritual meaning, and explain it.
    b. Read, afterwards, Tennyson's "Gleam;" what in this poem makes you think of King Arthur?
11. Read Arthur's farewell, line by line, asking what each sentence means with reference to Arthur's life. Which words in it best represent Arthur himself?

Arthur, the King:

12. When Arthur was crowned, what was his purpose in ruling?
13. What rules of conduct, what ideals of life, did he hold as guides for himself?
14. Who was his dearest friend? What was the condition and test of friendship with the king?
15. What did he expect of Guinevere, in the kingdom?
16. By what pledges did he bind the Knights of the Round Table?
17. What did he expect of his knights?
18. Who was the greatest of his knights?
19. Who among them was most loyal to the king?
20. Who of all the knights best understood Arthur's purpose? Percival speaks of not understanding all the king meant.

At the time of the battle in the west:

21. a. Where was Arthur's friend?
    b. What had become of the queen?

22. In what condition was the fellowship of the Round Table?
23. Did Arthur, when dying, believe that his life had been a failure?
24. Had the king's life really been worth living?

The Beauty and Meaning of Idylls of the King:

25. Of all in Idylls of the King, which passage do you care most for on account of the beauty that is in it?
26. In all the Idylls, what passage has brought to you the deepest and best meaning; that is, what passage would you care most to remember always for the influence of its meaning in your life? Written answers, with reasons, to hand in.

"THE PASSING OF ARTHUR" AS CONCLUSION OF THE ETHICAL SIGNIFICANCE OF IDYLLS OF THE KING.

For the circumstances attending the dedication of *Idylls of the King*, in 1862, to the memory of Prince Albert, see Memoir, vol. i., pp. 479, 480, 482, 485. "The Dedication" and "To the Queen," added in the volume of 1872 should be studied attentively in connection with the "Passing of Arthur." The "Dedication" expressed the deepest feelings of the poet's heart, and the parallel in his mind between the Prince Consort, gentle and beloved, and his king's ideal knight naturally led to a characterization which is, in reality, a comment on the Idylls. In "To the Queen," the poet returned to the same theme, asking his queen to accept this "old, imperfect tale, new-old, and shadowing sense at war with soul," not for itself but for the sake of one "to whom I had made it o'er his grave sacred."

1. Present in writing the most complete and significant expression you are able to make of Arthur's ideal for himself, his knights, his kingdom.

NOTE.— It is necessary to trace this ideal of the king through the Idylls, defining the special phase of it expressed in each. The written expression of it should, however, be original composition giving the individual impression and understanding of it; quotations should be used only in illustration.

2. Present from careful study of the Idylls the most complete and reasonable statement of the reasons or excuses of those who dissented from Arthur in his purpose, or who failed in the fulfillment of the obligations willingly assumed.
3. To what did Arthur himself attribute his failure to achieve his purpose?
4. *a.* In Tennyson's conception, what were the causes of the failure of the king's ideal?
   b. Where in the Idylls do you first find these causes of failure at work?
   c. Why did the king fail to understand the moral decay going on around him? At what time is the first sign of alarm or suspicion on his part?
5. What is the final word of the poet in regard to Arthur's ideal?
6. In what, chiefly, lay the tragedy of Arthur's life?
7. In the outward incidents at the close of Arthur's life, what elements of great tragedy are found?
8. By what means did the poet sink these to comparative insignificance in his narrative?
9. How long a time passed between the first writing of "The Passing of Arthur" and the addition of the lines which completed the poem? What evidence that Tennyson's purpose had changed, meantime, is contained in the poem itself?
10. *a.* What qualities of the Homeric style do you find in "The Passing of Arthur," as published in 1842?
   b. In what qualities, chiefly, do the lines written later differ from the earlier ones?
   c. What evidence, in the earlier poems, do you find foreshadowing an epic character in the series?
   d. In what respect did Tennyson modify or sacrifice epic qualities, and substitute other literary forms of expression?

NOTE.— This topic involves, first, a comparison of the literary qualities of the earlier and later poem, with a view of distinguishing essential differences, and, secondly, an inquiry as to the artistic requirement, in the poet's mind, fulfilled by each carefully chosen literary quality. It must be remembered that a slow change had taken place in the poet himself between 1842 and the completion of *Idylls of the King*, which also had its influence in the choice of artistic qualities.

11. What is the significance of Arthur's last words?
   a. In relation to the theme of the Idylls.
   b. As a revelation of Tennyson's philosophy of life.

NOTE.— The second point would be irrelevant in the critical study of *Idylls of the King* were it not that the ethical content of of these poems is intimately bound up with Tennyson's personal belief; his religious beliefs, his attitude of mind, a tendency to pessimism or the reverse, find expression in his writings, and one poem may serve in the interpretation of another. His attitude toward historic Christianity, however, must not be confused with his acceptance or rejection of the present expression, in the form of creeds, of beliefs descended from the mediaeval church.

CRITICAL STUDY OF IDYLLS OF THE KING.

General topics for critical study of *Idylls of the King* are omitted from this study. The suggestions given below are intended as an aid in the formation and expression of such critical opinion as has naturally resulted from the previous reading. The topics suggested occasionally in the Study-Guide may easily be made the subjects of extended and valuable critical study by individuals having leisure, aptitude, and library facilities at command.

In study clubs, written papers may be arranged, when desired, on topics suggested in the introduction, for note-book work; or, literary qualities, special topics, etc., may be selected as subjects of critical inquiry ; an original and valuable paper may be written by carrying out in all the Idylls, the study suggested in the single Idyll, for the single topic.

1. The relation of the Idyll to the series:
    a. "The Coming of Arthur": State fully, in your own words, discuss, and illustrate, the true subject or purpose of this Idyll as an act in the drama of the series.
    b. The following *momenti* run through the series; discuss the dramatic significance of each in "The Coming of Arthur," in relation to the subject of the Idyll, and the larger narrative of the series:
    (1) Arthur's secret word and ideal.
    (2) Guinevere's sin.
    (3) Lancelot's relation with the king and the strife of his inner life.
    (4) The corruption and decay of the Round Table, noting causes, progress, etc.
    (5) The state of the kingdom with reference to the fulfillment of Arthur's ideal.
    c. Discuss in the same way, "Gareth and Lynette."
    d. Discuss "Geraint and Enid," and "The Marriage of Geraint," as one Idyll.
    e. Discuss "Balin and Balan," as above, considering especially the significance of the Idyll as transition from the preceding Idyll to the "Merlin and Vivien."
    f. Discuss "Merlin and Vivien," considering the subject, and the *momenti* mentioned above.
    g. As above, consider "Lancelot and Elaine."
    h. As above, "Pelleas and Ettarre."
    i. "The Last Tournament," as above.
    NOTE.— Each Idyll should be considered as a continuation of all that have preceded, and at each point in the discussion the added significance of the motive, or act, in comparison with the same in previous Idylls is the point for attention.
    j. "Guinevere, as above, and with especial reference to the dramatic culmination and the conclusion of *Idylls of the King*.

II. The Idylls as a dramatic action in twelve parts:
    a. In what is the beginning of the plot:

b. In what is the climax?

c. What is the conclusion?

Show whether the great scenes in the spiritual content of the Idylls coincide with the dramatic scenes, and moments.

d. In what points did the ethical meaning modify or limit the dramatic presentation of the Idylls?

e. In what points did the necessity of the development of dramatic action limit or confuse the presentation of spiritual meaning?

f. What allegorical elements do you find in *Idylls of the King?*

g. What is the relation of the allegorical elements to the dramatic presentation? To the spiritual meaning of the Idylls?

NOTE.— A word must be said in regard to the allegory threading these Idylls. The author's own word of warning is important, for, in the pursuit of the fable, readers almost certainly miss some part of the subtle spiritual meaning it was intended to convey. A memorandum of Tennyson's earliest plan for "King Arthur" has been preserved and is given in chapter v. of volume ii. of the "Memoir." Hallam Tennyson in his note says "that the allegorical drift here marked out was fundamentally changed in the later scheme of the Idylls." In later years, the poet admitted the allegorical drift in the inner meaning of these poems but insisted that an allegory should never be pressed too far; —" I hate to be tied down to say this means that," he once answered, "because the thought within the image is so much more than any one interpretation."

III. The Reading of Criticism of Idylls of the King:

References for interpretation and criticism of *Idylls of the King* are given in the bibliography. These should be read for comparison of differing opinions. If it is desirable to assign topics for report, each reader or student should take a single topic, as "The Character of Arthur," or "The Allegorical Meanings;" and read many books on the single point. A report which consists of the statement and discussion of differing opinions of several writers will be of real value.

THE END.

The Study-Guide Series.

FOR USE IN HIGH SCHOOLS:

The Study of Ivanhoe. Third Edition. Map of Ivanhoe Land, plan of Conisborough Castle. Single copies, each, 50 cents. For use in classes, each, net, 25 cents.

A Guide to English Syntax. A practical study of syntax in prose text. Single copies, each, 50 cents. For use in classes, each, net, 25 cents.

The Study of Four Idylls of the King. Topics, notes, references, etc., for Gareth and Lynette, Lancelot and Elaine, The Passing of Arthur. Students' edition. Single copies, each, net, 30 cents. For use in classes, each, net, 20 cents; prepaid, 25 cents.

FOR USE IN COLLEGE CLASSES, STUDY CLUBS, ETC.

The Study of Romola. Arranged for study of the art of fiction in the historical novel and of the period of the Renaissance in connection with it.

The Study of Henry Esmond. Arranged for study of the historical period, the novel, characteristics of the author, etc.

The Creative Art of Ficton. A discussion of narrative art, plot structure, etc. Special price for use in classes.

The Study of Idylls of the King. Arranged for critical study of plot, dramatic unity of series, artistic and literary qualities, etc. Price. Single copies, each, 50 cents. Special price for use by classes, study clubs, etc., per copy, net, 40 cents.

Published by H. A. DAVIDSON, Cambridge, Mass.

IN THE RIVERSIDE LITERATURE SERIES.
WITH AIDS TO STUDY, BY H. A. DAVIDSON.

George Eliot's Silas Marner. No. 83. Paper, 30 cents; linen, 40 cents.
Oliver Goldsmith's Vicar of Wakefield. No. 78. Paper, 30 cents; linen, 40 cents.
Nathaniel Hawthorne's House of the Seven Gables. No. 91. Paper, 50 cents; linen, 60 cents.
The Vision of Sir Launfal and Other Poems. No. 30. Paper, 15 cents; linen, 25 cents.

Published by HOUGHTON, MIFFLIN & COMPANY, Boston.

Irving's The Sketch Book. Illustrated.

Published by D. C. HEATH AND COMPANY, Boston.

THE BORROWER WILL BE CHARGED
AN OVERDUE FEE IF THIS BOOK IS
NOT RETURNED TO THE LIBRARY ON
OR BEFORE THE LAST DATE STAMPED
BELOW. NON-RECEIPT OF OVERDUE
NOTICES DOES NOT EXEMPT THE
BORROWER FROM OVERDUE FEES.

Harvard College Widener Library
Cambridge, MA 02138   (617) 495-2413

CPSIA information can be obtained at www.ICGtesting.com
Printed in the USA
BVOW06s1044021215

429134BV00031B/402/P